ON TOP OF THE WORLD

ON TOP OF THE WORLD

Five Women Explorers in Tibet

Luree Miller

The Mountaineers · Seattle

THE MOUNTAINEERS: Organized 1906
"...to encourage a spirit of good fellowship
among all lovers of outdoor life."

© 1984 Luree Miller

Published by The Mountaineers
306 2nd Ave. W., Seattle, Washington 98119

First printing October 1984
Second printing June 1985

Published simultaneously in Canada by Douglas & McIntyre, Ltd.
1615 Venables Street, Vancouver, British Columbia V5L 2H1

Book design by Colin Lewis
Maps by Colin Lewis
Cover design by Marge Mueller

Manufactured in the United States of America

Library of Congress Cataloguing in Publication Data

Miller, Luree.
    On top of the world.

    Reprint. Originally published: New York: Paddington
Press, © 1976.
    Bibliography: p.
    Includes index.
    1. Explorers, Women.   2. Tibet (China) — Description
and travel.   I. Title.
[G200.M48 1984]   915.1'5043'0088042   84-16619
ISBN 0-89886-097-0

CONTENTS

To My Mother, Margaret Watson Smith:
An Inspired Traveler

> "When the mother image loses its
> sanctity, something will take its place
> on the altar. And any writer knows that
> when the image of the heroine changes,
> the plot changes with her."
>
> CATHERINE DRINKER BOWEN

AUTHOR'S NOTE

EVER SINCE I WAS ten years old and made my first trip east of the mountains—from Seattle to Weiser, Idaho—I have been enchanted by travel and tales of travelers. My mother, an artist with a romantic temperament, likes to claim she has some gypsy blood. My father, an educator, based much of his energetic career on the conviction that nothing contributed more to individual or international understanding than travel and cross-cultural friendships. I am grateful to both of them for imparting to me an enthusiasim for seeing the world, and to my husband for making it possible for me to do so. I have done most of my traveling with him—first in Alaska, his home state, then in Europe and Asia after he joined the Foreign Service. It was during our seven-year sojourn on the Indian sub-continent that I first heard tales of early Western women travelers to that part of the world and began to search for documentation about them.

In that search I incurred more debts than I am able to acknowledge, particularly in Asia. It is a very hospitable land. Numerous friends and strangers in India, Pakistan, Afghanistan, Sri Lanka,

Bangladesh, Nepal and Sikkim showed me many kindnesses and gave me valuable assistance.

My special thanks are due to my long-time colleague, Marilyn Silverstone, Magnum photographer and scholar of Tibetan culture, for enabling me to join her on a trip to Sikkim. We are indebted to His Highness the Chogyal of Sikkim and Her Highness the Gyalmo of Sikkim for their gracious hospitality and great generosity. Long conversations at the Palace in Gangtok (where I wondered if we were drinking from the same tea cups used by Alexandra David-Neel) were most helpful to my understanding of Tibetan Buddhism and the influence of Tibet on the Himalayan states. Thanks to their Royal Highnesses, Marilyn and I were able to travel to Sikkim like Edwardian ladies (though in jeeps rather than on ponies) with our cook, bearer, interpreter, and several other servants. Our table set up en route was always laid with white linen and proper china and cutlery. During our stay at the monastery of Pemayangtze (sometimes written Pemionchi) the monks showed us the same hospitality their predecessors had shown to Nina Mazuchelli in the 1870's and to Alexandra David-Neel in the early 1900's.

My greatest single debt of gratitude is to Mlle. Marie-Madeleine Peyronnet, secretary to the late Alexandra David-Neel. Mlle. Peyronnet generously allowed me to read and quote from the letters of Madame David-Neel, including the second volume (now in press) of her edited letters, and gave me numerous photographs. On two separate occasions she offered me the hospitality of the home in Digne, France, which she shared for so many years with David-Neel and which she now maintains, part of it as a museum. Mlle. Peyronnet gave me hours of her valuable time in person and by mail, answering a long series of inquiries. Her generous assistance and constant encouragement sustained me through the difficult task of sorting out the contradictions regarding David-Neel's life.

The problem with researching the other four women in this book was to find sufficient biographical sources. With David-Neel, however, there was an abundance of material: thousands of letters, piles of scrapbooks, trunks of clippings, boxes of pictures, and people who had known her to be interviewed. My old friend and world traveler, Valerie La Breche, drove me to the south of France and shared my search for the story of David-Neel. Many times she was my interpreter and intermediary and I am deeply indebted to her. She interviewed M. Gabriel Monod-Herzen when he returned from Pondicherry, India, after I left France, and she responded to all my transatlantic requests with tact and dispatch. I am indebted also to Scott Miller, who transcribed taped conversations, read and translated letters, and let me discuss with him the complexities of David-Neel's life and personality.

I want to express my particular gratitude to Professor and Mrs. William Sewell of Richmond, Surrey, England, for their recollections of life in West China during the 1920's when they were at Union College, Chengtu, Szechwan. Our conversation about David-Neel and the letter Professor Sewell kindly showed me, which he had written home after hearing Madame David-Neel lecture, were most helpful. Mr. John Robinson, formerly of the London publishers Rider and Co., was generous in his recollections of David-Neel as were many others who responded to my inquiries.

The brilliant lectures of Dr. Thelma Z. Lavine, Elton Professor of Philosophy, George Washington University, Washington, D.C., made me realize how much I have yet to learn about women and society's attitude toward them, and I thank her for reading and commenting on my first draft of David-Neel's life.

I am grateful to Julie Tonkin, University of Pennsylvania, for the delights of shoptalk about women travelers, and for bringing to my attention the Fanny Bullock Workman Traveling Fellowship at Bryn Mawr College. I want to thank Elizabeth Knowlton, biographer of Mrs. Workman for *Notable American Women*, for her kind and full response to my questions.

I owe a word of gratitude to friends in England: to Glorya Hale for making me write; to Judy Hillelson for introducing me to the pleasures of the open stacks at the London Library; and to John Hillelson, who shared my enthusiasm and helped me hunt for old books during the six years I lived in London. I want to thank

Chris Rosenfeld for helpful references she came across while doing her own research, and Joan Saunders for double-checking sources after I left London.

Peter Petcoff, Reference Librarian at the Library of Congress and my good neighbor, was unstinting in his assistance. I am grateful to Elizabeth Jenkins, also at the Library of Congress, for finding many lost books, and to Gary Fitzpatrick of the Library of Congress Map Division for his advice and help. I should like to acknowledge the assistance of the staffs of the Reading Room of the British Museum, the London Library, the India Office Library, the Bibliothéque Nationale, Paris, and particularly Mlle. Francoise Cousin in the Asian Department, Musée de l'Homme, Paris, who got from storage the boxes of David-Neel's Tibetan Collection, including the clothes she wore and the few possessions she carried on her journey to Lhasa. My thanks are due to Keith Snyder for typing my manuscript and to Rachel Johnson for her expert indexing.

My publisher, Janet Marqusee, and editor, Dick Ehrlich, have given me critical advice and constant encouragement from the inception of this book; I am most grateful to them.

Lastly, I must acknowledge my profound gratitude to my family—Stacy, Blair and Scott—for being such good travelers from the very beginning, and to Bill, who read and criticized my manuscript, and took me out to dinner.

There are many variations in the spelling of Tibetan and Chinese place-names. In most instances I have tried to adopt a standardized form rather than follow the different spellings used by the subjects of this book.

All quotations attributed to the five women are from their own writings. See full references given at the end of each chapter's footnotes.

INTRODUCTION

TALES OF ADVENTURE SINCE the time of Homer have glorified those daring men who disdained the safety of well-worn roads to discover what lay beyond the known world. They were heroes: brave, imaginative, resourceful, shrewd, and bedeviled by a curiosity that would not let them rest long in the confines of society. Underlying all the great sagas of exploration was an understanding that the impulse to roam and explore was masculine. The necessary complement to this understanding was the assumption that all women, because of their child-bearing ability, were creatures close to nature, and therefore content to remain enclosed in domestic life. There they waited, by the hearth, essential audiences for the returning heroes.

Then rather suddenly in the late 1800's, when women were laced into layer upon layer of cumbersome clothing and bound by strict Victorian codes of conduct, a small band of astonishing women explorers and travelers burst forth to claim for themselves the adventurous life. Among them were the five dauntless women who are the subject of this book: three British—Nina Mazuchelli,

Annie Taylor, and Isabella Bird Bishop; one American—Fanny Bullock Workman; and one French—Alexandra David-Neel.

These outriders of women's liberation were without exception romantics, restless with a desire to be up and away to unknown places. "What had I dared to dream. . . . Into what mad adventure was I about to throw myself?" Madame Alexandra David-Neel asked rhetorically as she began her walk—more than 2,000 miles—from China to Lhasa in Tibet.

For all of the women travelers of this period the individual gesture was supreme. They acted upon the impulse of their curiosity. Nothing in their temperaments or training prepared them for group action. The woman's suffrage movement launched in the mid-nineteenth century did not excite the imagination of any except Fanny Bullock Workman, who was an avowed suffragist. But neither she nor any of the others was caught up in this mainstream of feminine energy. Each woman was absorbed in her own dream, and each made her own journey without benefit of sponsorship.

Unaffiliated with any government, army, survey, or organization of importance, women travelers and explorers were allotted no places in standard history books. Only a few actually sought fame and set records. For most it was enough to have taken destiny in their hands, to have broken out of a dull or distasteful life and ventured forth to see with their own eyes the real world they had always learned about secondhand. Occasionally there is a passing reference to one of these self-reliant women in another traveler's book—to a Miss Christie inexplicably met in a Kashmiri valley or a single unnamed lady encountered in some outlandish corner of Arabia. But most women travelers were self-effacing to a fault. Few left accounts of their exploits. If they did, the record was apt to be a slim diary or letters written home and later privately printed in a book with gilt edges and tooled leather binding, full of charming sketches and competent watercolors. Today these books may turn up on the jumbled shelves of a used book store or in some family collection. These tantalizing bits of evidence attest to an intriguing but indeterminate number of singular women quite unlike either the submissive stereotypes of the late Victorian or Edwardian periods or the more organized, politically minded suffragists. But for the most part the early women travelers and explorers are shadows without substance.

Exceptions to this rule are a happy handful who did leave enough records to round out their lives. In that small group were Isabella Bird Bishop, Fanny Bullock Workman and Alexandra David-Neel, all of whom wrote a number of successful books and achieved sufficient fame to be saved from oblivion. The two other women considered here, Nina Mazuchelli and Annie Taylor, left only a single diary or book about the great experience of their lives.

The adventures of these five indomitable women demonstrated that they shared certain characteristics of the hero figure, qualities not often attributed to the feminine nature: a lively curiosity, calm judgment, practicality and courage. And, without exception, they proclaimed a *joie de vivre* seldom voiced by unconventional females in any age.

In the Victorian period, which was the last great age of exploration, some women were drawn to such exotic places as Arabia, Africa and the Gobi Desert. But wherever else they may have traveled, the strongest magnet that drew the five women in this book from the comfort and safety of home was Tibet.

With the British based in India it was inevitable that Westerners would develop a keen curiosity about the closed country on India's northern border. Politically, Tibet's frontiers were ill-defined. They stretched 1,600 miles from China to Kashmir and encompassed an area about three times the size of France. The great caravan route that Marco Polo had followed to the courts of Kubla Khan swung in an arc across the high plateau of Tibet's northern border. Its southern rim was secured by the awesome Himalayas, the highest mountains in the world—sharp jagged peaks rising straight from the populous plains of India. To the west was the great Karakoram mountain range. And sealed away behind these barriers at 16,000 feet was the forbidden land, the highest country in the world, unchanged by the swirl of history around it, a symbol of dreams and adventure.

Culturally, Tibet's influence extended further—into the Chinese provinces of Szechwan, Kansu and Yunnan; all along the Himalayas where, on occasion, the kingdoms of Nepal, Sikkim and Bhutan had paid tribute to Lhasa; and into the state of Ladakh, often called Little Tibet, west of the Karakorams in Kashmir. Traditionally the Chinese Empire had a nominal suzerainty over Tibet, but by the end of the nineteenth century its hold had weakened. The political vacuum left by China heightened the power struggle between Great Britain and Russia in Central Asia. Intrigue and speculation were rife. This imperialistic maneuvering, dubbed The Great Game, was immortalized by Rudyard Kipling in *Kim*. Popular magazines such as *Blackwell's, Cornhill, Cosmopolitan, Saturday Review, Scribner's* and *The National Geographic* published from the late 1800's on an increasing number of articles about this strange country. Christian missionaries, eager to proselytize, edged from India and China toward the Tibetan Buddhist stronghold of Lhasa. In 1891 the Smithsonian Institution in Washington, D.C., sent a scientific expedition to traverse the barren Tibetan plateau, but it did not reach Lhasa. Then in 1904 a small British Army Expedition under Colonel Francis Younghusband took the capital but soon withdrew. Tibet sealed its borders once more and remained mysterious and inaccessible.

For Madame David-Neel and Mrs. Bullock Workman the challenges of Tibet became the consuming passion of their lives. For the others it was a region of escape, however brief; a venue for self-expression and fulfilment, the perfect setting for the romantic adventure. To travel in Tibet was to transcend the limitations of sex. Some deep need for adventure and excitement must have impelled these women to explore the fringes of Tibet (and, in the cases of Annie Taylor and Alexandra David-Neel, to plunge to its heart). If they suffered any malaise of a psychological origin, as some of their contemporaries no doubt thought, they chose the anodyne of action rather than introspection—they seized their moments with an unselfconsciousness that would not be possible today. Danger gave zest to their lives and obstacles only strengthened their resolve.

"But here I am after long and patient waiting," wrote Nina Mazuchelli, as she, the first Western woman to do so, gazed at Mount Everest; "for it was the dream of my childhood to see this nearest point of earth to heaven." Annie Taylor, aflame with Christian zeal, made a wild dash over treacherous mountain passes to carry the Word to innocent Tibetans. And the lone traveler Isabella Bird Bishop sought the remote areas of Tibet simply to get away from it all, to take leisurely delight in the pleasures of solitary discovery. For the energetic American, Fanny Bullock Workman, Tibet offered mountains to climb, glaciers to explore, records to set. And Alexandra David-Neel found there a whole life, beginning in a cave in Sikkim where she lived for an entire winter as a hermit, and culminating more than a decade later when at last, in the disguise of a Tibetan beggar woman, she reached Lhasa. She was the first European woman to see the golden-roofed Potala, residence of the Dalai Lamas. Adventure, forever the prerogative of men, was what these women craved, and in varying degrees their dreams were realized.

The nineteenth and early twentieth centuries were the heyday of the British Empire and most of the Victorian travelers were the Queen's loyal subjects. Nina Mazuchelli went with her husband, a chaplain in Her Majesty's Indian Service, to Darjeeling, a station in the foothills of the Himalayas in Bengal. There, at the edge of her dreamed-of mountains she used her womanly wiles to organize a small expedition. Annie Taylor, a reckless, romantic missionary with the British Moravian mission in China, could not resist the pull of forbidden Tibet although she knew her life was in danger the moment she crossed its borders. The diminutive, determined Isabella Bird Bishop, an experienced traveler and successful writer, was nearly sixty years old when she went to Tibet. With different dreams but a common resolve to reach Tibet, these British women escaped from the closed-in feeling of a small, well-settled and neatly tended country, to travel in the uninhabited uplands of Asia.

America had its own frontier, still open to restless spirits. But New England-born Fanny Bullock Workman ignored the

Rocky Mountains and concentrated her formidable drive on the terra incognita of the great Himalayan and Karakoram mountains of Little Tibet. Fanny's expedition in 1912 was the largest and the only serious scientific expedition ever directed by a woman in that area before World War I. When the Great War put an end to exploration and travel, Fanny and her husband returned to Europe to write their last book. After the war a new era of exploration began—specially trained, well-equipped teams spread out to follow up the great Victorian travelers. The world map was divided up by geographical societies and mountaineering expeditions, and the days of the independent expeditions were over. Fanny never returned to the subcontinent.

It was the secrecy of Tibet that fired the curiosity of Madame Alexandra David-Neel, the French woman and Oriental scholar. "What decided me to go to Lhasa was, above all, the absurd prohibition which closes Tibet," she wrote. "I had sworn that a woman would pass the Tibetan frontier and I would." She longed to know the esoteric secrets of Tibetan Buddhism. Ablaze with what she called "the sacred fire of adventure," Alexandra David-Neel was the supreme romantic. Her ambitions surpassed those of any of the women who went before her. In the Tibetan Buddhist mysteries she transcended not only her sex but herself. The most amazing of them all, David-Neel was the last lone traveler to interior Tibet.

Although David-Neel's main journeys were made between the two World Wars, she was born in 1868 and grew up, like the other travelers, in a period when women were considered frail vessels whose bodies would be broken by strenuous exercise and whose minds would be shattered by excessive study. Most women believed in the contemporary medical wisdom and accepted its restrictive concepts. They suffered from heart palpitations and fainting spells, not realizing it was their tight corsets and stays that caused them pain. The sturdier travelers, one would surmise, shed their corsets as soon as they were clear of towns and villages. But they say maddeningly little about their personal concerns. Pictures of them show that they conformed to prevailing styles and wore skirts, at least when seen by others. None was an advocate of Amelia Bloomer's dress reform or Lady Harberton's Rational Dress Society. How they arranged their toilet and the inevitable complications of female hygiene without accustomed amenities remains a mystery.

Working-class women and farmers' wives toiling long hours and doing heavy manual labor had always belied the popular concept of female frailty. What was remarkable about the Victorian travelers was that, as middle- and upper-class women, they eschewed the role of the lady and rejoiced in their physical prowess. Fanny Bullock Workman devoted a chapter in one of her books to her fervid contention that any woman could climb mountains, even without any physical training, as she had. She did concede that her brief difficulty in breathing at 17,000 feet might have been prevented had she adjusted to higher altitudes in slow stages rather than going to the summits straight from the steamy plains. Isabella Bird Bishop had a tumor removed from her spine when she was a child and suffered all her life from a vague ailment. In letters to her sister at home in Edinburgh, Isabella innocently wondered why it was that she felt so marvelously well when she traveled, even in the most uncomfortable and primitive places, and invariably fell ill, often to be bedridden, shortly after returning home. It was Nina Mazuchelli, the only woman in her expedition, who urged the party on when they were lost on a glacier. Annie Taylor slept out in the snow at high altitudes. And David-Neel, carrying nothing more than a backpack and begging bowl, made her amazing eight-month trek through tropical lowlands and snow-covered passes when she was fifty-six years old.

Hardy as these women were, however, they did not imitate men or revolt against them. Four of the five were married. Nina Mazuchelli portrayed her husband lovingly—if a bit patronizingly—as a pipe-smoking, faintly obtuse male who could be managed. Late in life Isabella Bird made a happy marriage. And Fanny Bullock Workman's marriage was a harmonious and highly successful partnership. Only Alexandra David-Neel found matrimony confining, her dashing husband's *air mechant* a bit heavy for her taste. But they never divorced and he remained the fixed center of her nomadic life, her agent and the recipient of more than 3,000 of her letters. If Annie Taylor and Isabella Bird (before her marriage) had liaisons on their travels they were so discreet it is impossible to uncover any evidence. Affairs of the heart, in any case, were not the motivation; they all traveled not for the love of men, but for the love of adventure.

Yet they were ladylike wherever they went, their attitude no doubt emitting an awesome authority. With superb self-confidence they expected and received obedience from their male retainers. They saw no danger or impropriety in traveling alone with several men in their service. Perhaps they assumed that sex occurred only among equals—a quaint view confirmed by their experience. None of them was ever molested. Only Madame David-Neel reported one threatening situation, which she quickly had in hand. True, most of them were middle-aged when they reached Tibet, confident that gray hairs would be respected, and Mazuchelli and Workman had their husbands with them. But the others left the last tiny outposts of Asian civilization and gaily headed for the wilds to spend several months alone with a string of scruffy-looking male servants, usually a bearer, a cook, a groom and a coolie, about whom they knew practically nothing and with whom they could communicate very little if at all.

These five intrepid women are examples of the Victorian and Edwardian women travelers who covered the globe in an unprecedented burst of enthusiasm. The social and psychological obstacles they encountered were as formidable as the physical. But as they ventured into unknown regions they became inspired amateurs in the game of exploration. As women the world definitely was not their oyster. Nonetheless they sallied forth, in their proper long skirts and high-necked blouses, to pry open the shell a crack, to see for themselves if there were pearls in secret places.

How dull it is to pause, to make an end,
To rust unburnished, not to shine in use!

Tennyson
Ulysses

I. ENGLISH LADY TRAVELERS:

ELIZABETH SARAH MAZUCHELLI (1832-1914)

IT WAS THE HIMALAYAS that lured Nina into her rash venture. From the moment she had arrived in Darjeeling and gazed rapturously at the great mountain ranges she was filled with a longing to explore them. This was an unusual obsession for a mid-Victorian lady: such enterprises were the prerogatives of men. But Nina had an adventurous, even competitive spirit. "Several gentlemen had penetrated into the 'interior' by the direct route by which villages are frequently to be met," she declared, "but scarcely more than one European had traversed the crest of the Singaleelah chain, the route which we had marked for ourselves—and I was the first lady to explore the Eastern Himalaya by either way."

Elizabeth Sarah Mazuchelli, affectionately called Nina, had the true instincts of an explorer but her scope was limited. She was a lady. When she wrote an account of her expedition into the Himalayas titled *The Indian Alps and How We Crossed Them*, she deferred to the notion that a well-bred woman would not have her name in print, and signed her book anonymously: "By a Lady

Pioneer." What made Nina try to combine both worlds—that of the adventurer seeking new experiences, and that of the dutiful wife bowing to decorum—is not clear. There is no record of her early life.

The few facts that can be established about Nina are linked to her husband's history. A record in the India Office Library, London, indicates that Francis Mazuchelli, born 1820, and Elizabeth Sarah (no maiden name given), born 1832, were married in 1853. Francis was an Anglican parish priest who came, like most of the Anglican clergy, from the ranks of the upper class.[1] Four years after marrying Nina he left his position as curate in Wymering near Portsmouth, and joined the British army as a chaplain. The year was 1857, the date of the Indian Mutiny in which 70,000 Indian soldiers rebelled against the British. When Nina and Francis arrived in India the next year the uprising had been suppressed, but the illusion of British invincibility on the subcontinent was shattered. Even so, there was no breach of form in the proper Victorian society still maintained by the civilian and military rulers thousands of miles from home in an alien land. Calls were made, cards were left; all the social functions bound by a strict protocol went on as before.

This routine was wearisome enough at home where Queen Victoria set the somber standard, but surely more difficult to sustain for a young woman in a tropical country surrounded by a strange culture, the unintelligible gossiping of her servants, and the prying eyes of every villager.[2] Nina remembered vividly the delicious moment of release one day in 1869:

> We were sitting at dinner one evening beneath the pun-kah in one of the cities of the plains of India, feeling languid and flabby and miserable, when the "khansamah" [butler] presented Francis with a letter, the envelope of which bore the words, "On Her Majesty's Service"; and on opening it he found himself under orders for two years' service at Darjeeling, one of the lovely settlements of the Himalaya, the "Abode of Snow."

Were the "Powers that be" ever so transcendently gracious? Imagine, if you can, what such an announcement conveyed to our minds. Emancipation from the depleting influences of heat almost unbearable, for the bracing and life-giving breezes which blow over regions of eternal ice and snow.

In Darjeeling Nina's spirits soared. She developed a passion for galloping about the hills mounted side-saddle on her pony. Fast riding was "bad form," she admitted, but the keen mountain air made her disregard danger or propriety. An enthusiastic and very competent artist, she took her easel everywhere. Many Victorian ladies could draw and paint quite passably—such training was an important part of their limited education—but Nina considered herself a serious artist. For over a year she busily painted everything in sight and took daily horseback rides. But the Himalayas called her.

"The longing I had felt," she declared, "ever since my eyes first rested on that stupendous amphitheater of snow-capped mountains, ripened at last in such a strong determination to have a near view of them . . . that one evening as we were sitting cozily in Francis' sanctum, he smoking, and the fog literally trying to force its way through the keyhole, I cautiously broached the idea of a grand tour into the 'interior'."

Nina says that Francis registered extreme astonishment and, without taking his cigar out of his mouth, he replied, "I always knew, my dear—puff, puff—that it was useless—puff—to expect women—puff, puff—to be rational—puff, puff; but I never knew until this moment—puff—to what lengths you *could* go."

Nina, however, knew how to get her way. In her tone there was something of the spoiled child, a role dependent women often adopt if they are clever and attractive enough to manipulate their fathers or husbands. Very often, particularly in the Victorian period when patriarchy was at its peak, women's attitudes toward their husbands, and toward men in general, were shaped more by their relationship with their fathers than by any philosophical conviction about what men's and women's behavior toward each other should be. Since Nina apparently had no children herself, she may have more easily remained childlike in her attitude toward her husband, and he could afford to indulge her.

When Francis exploded at Nina's proposal to take an expedition into the Himalyas, she noted a certain twinkle in his eye at her audacity and knew "that I had only to keep up a judicious agitation, administered in small but frequent doses, to have my way in the end." And, she declared, "if these means did not answer, well then, I must make use of stronger measures, and bombard the citadel, for to go I was determined."

Nina and Francis at breakfast: ". . . faut de dish, we eat it with all due solemnity out of the frying-pan!"

Before Francis would capitulate to her plan he took her on a two-week trial trip into the hills to see if she could withstand camp life. To Nina it was an idyll in spite of the discomforts. At night the bats swooped down so close they fanned her cheeks. Water rats climbed the poles of the leaf hut she and Francis slept in, and noisily raided the provisions. But her characteristically English infatuation with animals inspired her to endow them all with human traits. Hearing "a tiny cadence" coming from a nest of mice near her head, she deduced, "They are evidently engaged in very animated conversation, our invasion being probably the subject of it," and she was eager for a look at "these interesting little pilgrims of the night."

Enraptured by the wilderness, Nina found everything beautiful beyond description. The storms that drenched her to the skin moved her to proclaim herself a lover of the passionate in nature. Rising at dawn she was delighted by the ethereal quality of the early morning light. When the sun came out she threw herself down on a soft carpet of ferns to watch the gorgeous butterflies, bees, and dragon flies. She dreamed she resembled the Lady of the Lake with flowing hair, but Francis did not seem to be a Sir Walter Scott hero. "We sally forth," she wrote, "Francis shouldering his gun and I his butterfly net." She declared herself a child of nature, and reveled in her unaccustomed freedom, thankful that "No solemn garden parties or funereal dinners, no weary conventionalities of society, follow us here."

Back in Darjeeling after passing her first test in the hills, Nina was advised by anxious friends to give up so rash an undertaking as her proposed expedition. "Many were the predictions," she said, "that even if Francis returned alive, I, at any rate, should leave my bones to whiten on some mountain-top." But her zest was only heightened by opposition, and she began to make preparations. Nina emphasized that "no lady had hitherto attempted to explore the Eastern Himalaya." She intended to travel "towards Mount Everest and Kanchenjunga—the two highest mountains in the world," explaining that "the perpetually snow-clad mountains of the Kanchenjunga group, it must be understood, form an impassible barrier, incapable of being crossed; it is, therefore, our intention to cross the range of intervening Alps till we reach their base, and then explore the glaciers."

At the time there were no detailed maps of the area and Nina was imprecise about the route her expedition took. Generally, according to her own rough map, the party traveled west from Darjeeling through low-lying valleys for about twenty miles, then climbed to the summit of the southern end of the Singalila mountain range, which Nina dubbed the Indian Alps. This range, with peaks from 10,000 feet to over 12,000 feet, runs roughly north and south, perpendicular to the Himalayas. Nina's expedition traveled along its crest toward Mount Kanchenjunga (spelled Kinchinjunga by Nina) in Sikkim and Nepal, until they reached Junnoo Mountain (25,311 feet) on the southern rim of the Himalayas. Their return was along the same route for nearly three-quarters of the way. At Mount Singalila (Nina's Mount Singaleelah, 12,366 feet) they turned east about thirty miles to Pemionchi, one of Sikkim's largest monasteries, and then followed the Great Rangit River (Rungheet to Nina) back to Darjeeling. By their own estimate they covered twelve to fifteen miles a day, six days a week. All told the distance they traveled was about 600 miles in two months' time.

A friend whom Nina identified as C. asked to join the expedition, offering to take charge of the commissariat. C. was a district officer, that unique official of the British Imperial Government in India who was, in one person, an executor, legislator and judge for his district. (A district might be more populous than a small country in Europe.) Nina described C. as "a mighty potentate in the eyes of the province, whose destinies he ruled with mild and beneficient sway." She did not name the province or district.

Wherever he came from, C., and Nina and Francis as well, seemed to be unaware of the political climate of the Himalayan frontier area or of the "Great Game" Britain and Russia were playing in Central Asia. When Queen Victoria was proclaimed Empress of India in 1876, it was to reaffirm and symbolize British power, not only to India but to Russia, whose influence in the highlands of Asia Britain feared. Indian territory and Tibet were contiguous for five or six hundred miles and northern military stations such as Darjeeling were seething with intrigue. Darjeeling itself and a sizeable slice of the little Himalayan kingdom of Sikkim had been annexed by the British in retaliation for the capture, torture and near starvation of two Englishmen who had entered the Rajah of Sikkim's territory on a botanical expedition.[3] And the Tibetans knew that the British trained an elite corps of natives, "pundits," as they were popularly called, to explore and gather information.[4] It was no wonder that all travelers beyond the imperial frontier were suspected of being spies or resented as foreign intruders. Yet Nina persuaded her husband to make this expedition into Sikkim where Britain and Tibet had clashed for years with rival claims of suzerainty. And with seemingly perfect confidence, C. made arrangements with two agents of the Rajah of Sikkim, the Kajee and the Soubah. (The Kajee was the Minister of State for Sikkim, the same one who had captured the unfortunate Englishmen. The Soubah was a sort of prince or viceroy.) They were to deliver food and supplies to prearranged points once the expedition crossed the frontier into the Rajah's territory. Through the combined treachery of these men Nina's expedition was led astray in one of the wildest regions in the world.

The expedition consisted of Nina, Francis, C., and about seventy servants: baggage coolies; a corps of sappers—men to cut and clear the path; cooks and their helpers; bearers to supervise setting up and breaking camp, serve table and attend to the sahibs' personal needs. "I did not intend to take a maid with me," Nina said, "although I anticipated great inconvenience in the absence of one. I believed I had no right to subject another woman to the hardships of the road and climate to which I had voluntarily committed myself."

For all of her adventurous spirit, Nina remained a lady. She never thought of compromising accepted standards of dress— and Victorian ladies' dress in the seventies was not conducive to vigorous movement, least of all mountain climbing. Women were literally weighted down and bound tight by clothes. Nina would have worn a chemise and drawers reaching to her knees, and a minimum of two petticoats, one probably flounced to the waist to give her skirt the voluminous shape shown in the sketches she made of herself to illustrate her book. These flounced petticoats became fashionable about 1866 as a replacement for the crinolines that were stiffened with metal or whalebone hoops. The corset was *de rigueur*; and the twenty-one-inch waist was an ideal some-times realized by tight lacing and grim forbearance. Nina's draw-ings of herself show her to be slim but not with an hourglass figure. Over the corset a camisole or petticoat bodice was worn, and sometimes a vest as well. Then came the dress, full-skirted to the floor and "considered to be a fit when a lady can neither raise her arms nor use her legs." A hat was always worn out-of-doors, with, if needed, a coat or shawl—certainly adding up to considerable poundage. And all supported by feet pinched into high-heeled boots. Francis, however, "conceived of the very original idea," Nina wrote, of her wearing "mocassins," as they would be warm and comfortable. That she agreed to wear them, Nina declared, proved her total lack of female vanity. But to walk any distance was out of the question.[5] Nina accomplished the journey of her dreams in a Barielly dandy.

A Barielly dandy she described as "a kind of reclining chair made of cane, and suspended by leather straps to a strong rim of wood, the shape of a boat, with a pole at each end." It was carried by four men at a time who were relieved at frequent intervals. Nina suffered a good deal of battering and shaking in the dandy and on steep ascents was knocked against sharp rocks, first in one direction, then another. Occasionally she became stuck between fragments of fallen rocks and the bearers would help her "alight with a gentleness as if they thought I would break, or in some other way fall to pieces." Indeed she must have seemed a preposterous creature to the hillsmen who carried her, accustomed as they were to seeing their own women bearing loads nearly as heavy as the men. In the dense jungles of bamboo, Nina wrote, "where we cannot see a yard before us," and "the whole is dark and vault-like, each cane being covered with a damp moss," where "not a bird or insect seems to live," she took "care to make my bearers keep well up with the gentlemen, for the gloom is painfully oppressive, and I would fain not be alone." At a nearly perpendicular precipice of 600 feet, the gradient was too steep for the dandy to be carried up and Nina was fastened in a bamboo chair with a strap encircling her waist. Then the chair with her in it was carried up on the back of a coolie, "with a whole staff of dandy-wallahs arranged before and behind me in case of accident." With such an insistence on her own physical fragility it is amazing that Nina persisted in a desire to explore unknown regions.

Nina, strapped into her chair, being carried up a mountain slope.

When the day of departure came, Nina stood at the window of her house in Darjeeling and watched the coolies leaving with their loads of baggage. "My pulse beat fast, and my heart throbbed; not, however, from the proud anticipation that we were about to travel amongst the most extensive mountains of the world, but— shall I confess it?—from misgivings lest, after all, the prophets of evil should be right, and I prove incapable of sustaining the fatigue of such a journey."

The hardships of travel were mitigated by extensive equipment —tents, tables, chairs, carpets, iron bedsteads, stoves, lamps, and china. Everything folded for transport on coolies' backs. Setting up camp produced a terrific hubbub—seventy men scurrying about in seemingly hopeless confusion, the Babel of different languages; and then, like a miracle, the tents were pitched and furnished, the carpets laid in them, stoves lighted, and the kettles boiling. The expedition's cow provided fresh milk for tea and some of the live chickens they carried with them were turned into what Nina called "sudden death" dinners.

The servants engaged for the expedition were native to the hills, coming from the tribal groups generally identified at that time as Lepchas, Bhootia, Nepaulese, and Sikkimese. Nina, Francis, and C. found these tribal people quite different from the Indians of the plains. "With our conventional English notions concerning the bearing of the lower classes to the upper," Nina reported, "it takes some little time to accustom ourselves to the familiarity of these hill men, and to their noisy behavior towards each other in our presence."

Breaking camp was a slower process. Nothing could induce these independent hillsmen to strike tents and be ready to march before 10 a.m. at the earliest. Nina, Francis and C. were up at dawn, had their tea and sent the sappers ahead to clear paths or make some where none existed. Then Nina would set off in her dandy to find some vista where she would sketch and paint until the rest of the expedition caught up with her. Francis and C. had to remain in camp to see that it was broken up and the coolies set on their way with their loads; otherwise the camp would not arrive by the end of the day's march.

Once the expedition had marched a few days out of Darjeeling and crossed into that part of Sikkim governed by the Rajah, there were no roads or even pathways to follow on the route they had set for themselves. Ponies were no longer practical and the three Europeans switched to their pre-arranged plan of travel, "I in my dandy," said Nina, "and the gentlemen walking." Without detailed maps they had to follow their instincts and trust to the configurations of the mountains. The terrain was made up of great heights and deep-cut ravines. One ridge was so narrow they could see the valleys, two thousand feet below, on either side. They marched from the scorching heat of the valleys into rain forests, where the almost perpetual cloud and vapor hung on the treetops, causing them to drip with moisture.

Some nights they were beset by insects attracted by the light of their lamps: flying ants, green locusts three inches long, and others Nina could not identify but which looked to her "like fat little men with their hands in their pockets." While C. read aloud to Nina and Francis they all tried to ignore the insects crawling up their sleeves, down their necks, and floundering in Nina's hair. She watched "the movements of one big fellow, on the light fantastic toe, pirouetting before me continually, as though he were performing for my especial amusement."

At 11,000 feet the expedition began to feel the cold. The summit of the Singalilan range they estimated to be about 12,000 feet. Here, beyond the timber line, the streams were frozen and the thin air intoxicating. Through a mishap they lost their aneroid thermometer and other scientific instruments so all measurements were guesswork. But they knew they would be climbing higher once they reached the glacier fields, so at this point they sent back a dozen or so coolies with camp bedsteads and some of the heavier furniture. Nina began to feel an oppressive sense of isolation. It was "utterly hopeless," she wrote, "to convey to the minds of those who have never traveled in the interior of the Himalaya, the almost fierce majesty and barren grandeur of Nature in this great lonely land. I have visited most of the mountainous districts of Europe," she explained, "but they give not the faintest idea of the wild desolation of these regions at 14,000 or 15,000 feet, commanding views of peaks twice their height again." Nina affirmed her adherence to the romantic view that being close to nature improved one morally. "As I stand in these vast solitudes I do so with bent knee and bowed head, as becomes one who is in the *felt* presence of the Invisible."

One night she crept out of the tent and climbed to a nearby

ridge with her drawing block and chalks to sketch Mount Kanchen-junga in the moonlight. "The very beauty of the scene made me afraid," she confessed; "it was all so supernatural, so pale, so still, so passionless, so spectral." Suddenly a sensation came over her as if she were being enveloped in a wet sheet: she was surrounded in fog so dense it blotted out all moonlight. She could see nothing but blackness. Cold and clammy, fighting down her impulse to call for help, she waited an eternity in the darkness, hearing noises, fancying moving shapes, until the cloud at last passed and she groped her way back to camp.

Another time the treacherous fog separated her and her dandy-bearers from the men; she heard their voices come near her and then retreat. It was, she said, "a fitting occasion for hysterics, but I am not given to such demonstrations."

If there was not the fog there was wind and rain. During one storm the wind cut and slapped their faces, howled dismally and chilled them to the bone. Its force was so great it knocked the coolies down and they staggered beneath their loads like drunken men. Nina sat inside the leaking tent under her umbrella and C. appeared, dripping wet, to offer her some cognac. "Nothing is farther from my intention, however," Nina declared, "than taking cold or allowing myself to be miserable."

The coolies said rain meant snow ahead and the sappers bolted. The chief cook got a fever and the cow refused to give milk. But more disastrous than all of that, the Soubah of Sikkim failed to appear with the promised supplies.

After several days of anxious waiting he at last arrived with the provisions. Nina was enchanted with him. She described him as the "*prettiest* and the most benevolent old man possible." He reminded her "of one of Rembrandt's glorious pictures, mellowed by time; and were one told that he had been sitting and smoking himself over the fire for a thousand years, one would scarcely feel surprised." The Soubah, in turn, was fascinated by Nina; he had never seen an Englishwoman before. To commemorate this meeting he ordered three stone slabs to be erected at the edge of the small lake where the expedition was encamped. The slabs looked like "Druidical remains," Nina wrote.

The large one in the center represents C., as becomes the greater dignity of his social position; that to the right Francis, and the little fat stumpy one looking like an excrescence, myself, which I feel slightly inclined to resent, being, I beg to say, neither fat nor stumpy; but then in this country a woman is nothing socially, a "*koosh nae,*" which being interpreted means *nothing.*

I am by no means one of those strong-minded females who advocate what is mis-called "woman's rights"; on the contrary, I believe women have tenderer, sweeter, purer, if not nobler, rights than such advocates wont of—rights best suited to the gentler nature of her sex, and hidden deep in the sweet and gentle life of home; but there are limits to the depreciation of womankind in the social scale, and on behalf of my Oriental sisters I object to the above order of ideas.

The Soubah consulted with C. over the route the expedition should take toward Mount Everest and gave them one of his own men as a guide. The expedition, replenished with supplies from the Soubah, pushed on. One morning several days later, Nina, in her usual fashion, took her drawing block and colors out to sketch when suddenly it dawned on her that she was gazing on Mount Everest, the highest mountain in the world. She rushed to a higher promontory where she had a better view. Clad from head to toe in fur, she worked hurriedly for an hour. "Still sketching away in a perfect heaven of wonder and delight," she wrote, "I am suddenly brought to earth by Francis, who, having discovered my whereabouts, and folding my rug more closely round my shoulders, enquires whether I have not gone mad, to remain thus in the cold before the sun is well up." He brought her back to camp and made her drink coffee with cognac in it, while Nina pleaded to be allowed to hurry ahead up the mountain to a point where she could make a more careful sketch of Mount Everest before clouds covered it. But nothing would induce Francis to give his consent; he remained absorbed in his cigar. Nina nevertheless persisted, knowing that "Importunity and 'agitation' at length prevail, as they always will over those who love peace and quiet" (which Francis apparently did). Finally he gave in and sent her up the mountainside in her dandy.

Francis was not always so pliant. After one particularly difficult day when the march was over rocky bluffs at about 14,000 feet and through narrow gorges where the icy wind whipped like a stinging lash, Nina was exhausted. She was so chilled and frozen that she finally buried her head in her lap, crying. Francis found her and insisted on her rousing and "eating dinner like a Christian." Nina wanted only to be left alone, but "finding that continued obstinacy would vex him," she decided "to make an effort."

Francis, like most Victorian Englishmen, felt that irregular habits were demoralizing if not altogether sinful. He insisted on dining—even in torrential downpours, bitter cold, and high altitudes—"with all due propriety and the preliminary solemnities which usually accompany an Englishman's dinner, be he where he may." The table was properly set with a cloth, china, and a lamp in the center, and served by the usual complement of bearers. At 14,000 feet, Nina related, "we dine in our hats and wraps—assembled round the dinner table and are so frightfully rheumatic, that when seated we don't know how in the world to get up again, and when standing it is a positive agony to think of sitting down."

After dinner the two men drew chairs toward the stove to smoke their cigars and drink their wine. Nina did not expect to be included in this ancient male ritual, and since she was the only Englishwoman in the mountains she could not retire with the ladies. So she read or wandered about the camp, she said, "like an unquiet ghost."

On Sundays they did not travel. Francis read the prayers and C. the lessons and psalms.

But as they climbed higher it became more difficult to maintain proprieties. The three Europeans no longer undressed for bed, but slept, as their servants always did, fully clothed. If they removed their clothes the garments froze. Meals were cut back to fewer courses. The nefarious Kajee reneged on the promised supplies of food, and the basic ration, rice, was diminishing ominously.

At this juncture Nina, Francis and C. realized that the expedition was in a dangerous situation. They had traveled the length of the Singalilan Range and were in utterly unknown country where the average elevation was around 14,000 feet. It was impossible to camp here and wait for the arrival of provisions from the Kajee as they had from the Soubah at a lower elevation. And at this point it would have been farther to Pemionchi, the monastery near the only village of any size that they knew about and had planned to visit on their return trip, than to Yangpoong, a village where, the guide assured them, they could replenish their food stocks. C. dispatched runners back to the Kajee demanding he deliver their provisions posthaste, and the expedition toiled forward.

By now they were in a region of ice and snow, eerily silent and desolate. Everyone felt the effects of the rarified atmosphere. The baggage coolies suffered from nausea and giddiness. Francis and C. had splitting headaches. Nina experienced heart palpitations and difficulty in breathing, "a distressing sensation," she said, "which has prevented my lying down for several nights past, obliging me to retain an upright position." In this awkward posture her long hair uncoiled and froze. When she woke it was standing out stiffly. She had to thaw it over a campfire before she could comb it.

Snow began to fall but the Soubah's guide led them on. Nina's exhausted dandy-bearers told her it was not the way to Yangpoong. "Go back to Darjeeling, mem sahib," they pleaded. "This is a cold, hungry country. No rice, no birds; nothing to eat here; we shall all be starved." But the guide assured the Englishmen that food from the Kajee would catch up with them. Then a messenger from the Kajee arrived with news that the necessary stores would be awaiting their arrival in Yangpoong. When Francis and C. objected, protesting that the supplies were not to be delivered to Yangpoong, the messenger replied that they should have no doubts; the Kajee would not play them false or show them any uncivility—

.... Nina Mazuchelli's route

he knew it would cost him too dear, "for he had a lively recollection of the retributive justice of the British Government."

Nina and Francis, however, were not so sanguine; they began to suspect treachery. But they were at the mercy of the Soubah's guide and soon were forced to go on a famine diet. Medicine ran out. Their faces were blistered and swollen, their lips livid and cracked; Nina described their complexions as a "mixture of blue and red like mottled soap."

After several days of excruciating progress over ice and new snow, the guide directed the expedition on a zig-zag ascent of a steep mountain face, with the promise that they would reach Yangpoong at the end of the day's march. Spirits raised, they started off, carefully following the footsteps of the guide in the deep snow. Several coolies fell into holes and with difficulty were dragged out. Everyone slipped and slid and at one ridge the bearers converted Nina's dandy into a makeshift sledge. Francis lost his footing and tumbled to the bottom of the slope. The glare of the snow tortured their eyes, a mist making the light intolerably dazzling. C. became blinded and had to be led by a coolie until, overcome with vertigo as well, he sank down in a state of utter collapse. The mist thickened into fog so dense that the guide and baggage coolies at the head of the expedition became separated from Nina, Francis and C. Numbed with fear, they could not tell how long they awaited for an answer to their shouts. At length the guide and coolies came straggling back, the guide announcing that he did not know the way to Yangpoong.

At this revelation, near-panic spread through the expedition. The Lepcha coolies dropped their loads, sank down on the snow and, in mute despair, buried their faces in their hands. But not the Bhootias, Nina reported. "With looks bold and defiant, [they were] talking together, but not low enough to prevent our hearing that they were blaming *us* for having brought them hither, 'where,'" as they said, "'they must starve and die,' not seeming to realize that we ourselves were in the like danger. Nor did they hesitate to imply that we had so brought them."

"At that moment," Nina wrote, "we were completely in their

power, and had they chosen, the whole camp might have broken out into open mutiny." Francis and C. held a desperate conference. The guide was adamant; he could not lead them on. The men considered sending several detachments of coolies in different directions to find camping grounds where there was wood, but discarded the plan as too risky. They deliberated over whether to go on or camp where they were, without wood, and wondered if tent-pegs would hold in the snow. A snowstorm was threatening. Nina recalled her feelings: "To travel further into the lonely heart of these mountains with the mere possibility of discovering our whereabouts, or lingering where we were on the miserable chance of the mist clearing would alike be running a tremendous risk. I felt that not an instant should be lost.

" 'Let us return at once; don't hesitate for a moment,' I cried, stamping the snow with my foot in my vehemence. 'It is the only thing to save us.' "

After a few moments of solemn and earnest consultation Francis and C. agreed.

"For one instant," Nina said, "a terrible pang shot through me. Was I destined to be the means of bringing sorrow on others? *I would come*: these three words pierced my very soul like a red-hot iron. Had I been less anxious the expedition would not have been undertaken at all. I thought of C.'s wife and his little children; I thought too of my mother and her letter of warning, on being informed of our proposed tour: 'I dread your traveling in a mountain region so little known to Europeans, and so far removed from civilization. Do not attempt too much. . . .' "

Francis and C. exercised all the authority they could muster to persuade the Bhootias and Nepalese to shoulder their loads and start back. Nina told how she went "amongst the baggage coolies—with my own hands I helped some to lift their loads, endeavoring at the same time to arouse others who had relapsed into a state of lethargy, trying to speak words of comfort and encouragement to all; feeling that if *I*, a woman, set the example of exertion, there was enough chivalry existing in the hearts of these poor creatures to make them not only obey but help me."

Painfully, some with feet cut and bleeding, the demoralized and desperate expedition staggered and straggled back down the mountain. The mist grew less dense and at length Nina sighted about two miles distant the great rock where they had camped the night before. From her dandy she set up the shout, "We are saved!"

Once the rock was safely reached, just as darkness set in, Nina gave up her brave front. A blinding pain throbbed in her head. Her eyes were so inflamed and eyelids so swollen she could scarcely see. She slumped down on a stone and leaned against a coolie's basket. C., now able to see a bit, fetched a bottle of chloroform, saturated a handkerchief with it and placed it across Nina's forehead and temples.

That night the guide disappeared, confirming their worst fears. They realized they should never have trusted the Kajee and Soubah. All that was left to feed themselves and nearly sixty men were two sheep and a few handfuls of corn, some tea biscuits and a little rum. These C. portioned out as they made forced marches, even on Sundays, back along their own trail. The three Europeans were very conscious of the hostility of the Bhootias and Nepalese in their expedition. Nina recalled the experience of one of her friends in Darjeeling whose Bhootia cook was thought to have slipped little doses of poison in the Englishman's tea. When accused, the cook retorted, "Do you think, Sahib, if we wanted to get rid of you we should resort to such small means as that? Ooh! we should cut your heads off at once."

Fortunately the Lepchas and Sikkimese were not belligerent. "As long as mem sahib keeps well," one of her dandy-bearers told Nina, "everyone will be brave, but if she gets ill, all will give in."

Nina was oppressed by terrible feelings of responsibility. She tore her garments into bandages, spread them with cold cream and bound wounds on the coolies' feet and legs. Some had such severely inflamed eyes they had to be blindfolded and led. C. continued to send messengers with entreaties for supplies to both the Soubah and the Kajee. "Disappointed hopes come each day with a cruel and terrible persistency," Nina said. Not one messenger returned. "Anxiety seems to be the litany of our lives."

A young coolie fainted and lay face down in the path. Nina found a little port wine in her traveling bag to revive him. Her dandy-bearers no longer had the strength to carry her. Nina began to walk, "with Francis' assistance."

C. decided to go ahead with a few coolies and gave them permission to sack any village they might come to along the way. Nina, "feeling that I was myself breaking down, and should soon be unable to proceed another step," summoned "the strongest of my bearers, and urged them to carry me, if but for a short distance." They entered an all but impenetrable forest; the rock was covered with black, slimy lichens. The only sound in the chilling air was the groans of the coolies—until all at once distant shouts were heard. It was C. returning with the news that supplies from the Kajee were coming. The coolies shouted, "Hurrah! No more dying, food has come." And the dandy-bearers in their excitement gave Nina a toss in the air, "the last effort of which I fancy they were capable," she wrote, "and then allowed me to follow the laws of gravitation unaided, and find my own level on the ground."

Fires were built on the spot and were ready by the time the Kajee's men arrived with baskets of food for the famished expedition. Overcome with relief, Nina and Francis sat on a fallen tree, unable to speak, scarcely able to eat.

Slowly, normal camp life resumed as more provisions were procured in the villages they passed through. If the villagers were reluctant to part with their goats, chickens or rice, C. simply brandished his rifle, but he always paid in silver for whatever he confiscated. Nina insisted, "we are a just and generous people."

They pitched their tents and opened long-forgotten boxes. Francis overhauled his bird and insect collection, so long neglected. C. cleaned his gun, Nina noted, "examining it lovingly and tenderly as men do." Nina got out her needle and thread to mend the holes in the canvas tents made by the coolies when they were in the mountains, trying to beat off the frost which accumulated each night and added so greatly to the tents' weight. "In short," Nina concluded, "all suddenly awaken—now that our troubles are over —as to a new life, feeling once more that the trifles of existence are worth attending to, and concern us still."

Their route to Pemionchi took them through the Kajee's village, and they met "the old ruffian." He received his English visitors on a knoll above his house. He was seated on a carpet with three piles of silk cushions in front of him for his guests. C., as a district officer and therefore of superior rank to Francis, was placed in the center on the highest stack of cushions. Pleasantries were exchanged and protocol observed.

The villagers all along their way were agog at this procession led by three fair-skinned, strangely dressed foreigners. Many of the women and children were so terrified they ran and hid. "An Englishman may possibly have been seen within memory of the 'oldest inhabitant,'" Nina explained, "but the genus Englishwoman, never."

The Tibetan Buddhist monks at the Pemionchi monastery gave the expedition a cheery welcome. Francis and Nina were charmed and grew quite fond of the monks in the few days they spent with them. The monks invited their English guests to a religious ceremony. C. abstained on religious grounds, but Nina and Francis attended the ancient Tibetan Buddhist rites.

Strange as were the surroundings of these pagans [Nina wrote], and grim as were their symbols, how can I find language to express the majesty and grandeur of their worship, which impressed me more deeply than anything I have ever seen or heard, and in which I realized faintly a sort of abstract idea of what the worship of the all-Supreme by poor feeble human lips should be? It filled me with wonder and admiration; and the chanting of their Service is a thing never to be forgotten while memory lasts.

This is scarcely the reaction one would expect from the wife of a Victorian Anglican chaplain.

An old woman at Pemionchi told Francis that Nina "looked

very *good*," and she hoped he did not beat her too much. Francis replied that "although it was the custom in India for men to beat their wives, in England it was all the other way!" This information was translated to the group of women who had gathered round. Nina recalled that the statement "was received by my feminine audience with a chorus of very feeling applause; and I think they not unwillingly would have migrated with their lords to that delightful country, to have a little revenge."

Nine would have liked to linger at Pemionchi but the expedition had to keep its schedule to receive the ponies that were being sent from Darjeeling to meet them at the Sikkim border. They crossed the Rangit River and were back in British Indian territory. That night Francis, C. and Nina sat over their last campfire reminiscing, loath to have the expedition end. Even their near-disaster on the mountain quickly became a memory to treasure. How odd it would seem, Nina lamented, "to return to the ways of civilization and to home duties, to receive a daily newspaper and daily letters, to have a roof between us and the sky, to live in a house with windows in it, to return visiting cards and '*burra khanas*,' to toilets and morning callers, and to be obliged to wear one's hair up, and to look spick and span and ladylike once more!"

Still, it would never be quite the same again. Nina and the gentlemen mounted their ponies and all along the way as they rode home, people came out of their huts and shops, and stopped work in the fields, "for they know," Nina wrote proudly, "that we have been over into Sikkim, and have left our footprints on the mighty snows, and we are something to look at after that."

It was an experience qualified to stir yearnings for immortality. Nina wrote her book protesting that it was intended for "the exclusive perusal of a family circle," based as it was on letters sent home to her mother, "during almost the only time we were ever separated."

Little else is known about Elizabeth Sarah Mazuchelli. She wrote one other book, *Magyar Land* (1881) about her trip in the Carpathian Mountains in central Europe. But *Crockford's Clerical Directory*, the standard reference where her husband's biographical data are found, did not and still does not recognize the existence of wives—perhaps due to a feeling that celibacy is the proper state for clergymen. Francis returned to civilian life in 1875, three years after Nina's expedition, and after eighteen years of service in India. He served in several English parishes until he settled in Wales, where he died in 1901 at the age of eighty-one. Presumably Nina, the vicar's wife, was with him in all those quiet parishes. Her will was filed at Nantgaredig, Carmarthenshire, Wales, where she died at the age of eighty-two years in 1914.

The careful, cultivated way of life on a little island must have seemed confining to Nina when she returned home. In the introduction to *The Indian Alps and How We Crossed Them*, written in 1876, one year after she was back in England, Nina confessed: "I am seized with a spirit of unrest and long to be far away and once more in their [the Himalayas'] midst." For one brief moment she had left the hearth and found the wide world exhilarating.

How many more Victorian women shared Nina's sentiments will never be known. The wives, daughters and sisters of Englishmen in exile were blamed for isolating their men from the real life of Asia.[6] No doubt they did. They were trained to protect the purity and sanctity of domestic life and to believe in their own fragility. But some of them must have been fired by their exotic surroundings and longed as much as any man to break with the staid social patterns into which they were locked. There were few ways a woman could experience the thrill of risk and feel of adventure as fully as Nina had. Yet when as unlikely a woman as Nina found a way, and proved to have the courage and determination of an explorer, others must have too. But women seldom wrote books. Without hers Nina would be one of those countless ladies lost to history.

Give to me the life I love,
Let the lave go by me,
Give the Jolly heaven above
And the byway nigh me.

Robert Louis Stevenson
"The Vagabond"

I. ENGLISH LADY TRAVELERS:

ANNIE ROYLE TAYLOR (1856-?)

AT DAYBREAK ON SEPTEMBER 2, 1892, as soon as the inner gate of the Chinese city of Tauchau was unlocked, a small round-faced Englishwoman and her servant crept past the sleepy guards and hurried through the outer gate to meet another servant outside with the horses. At a pre-arranged meeting place they joined a Chinese guide and his Tibetan wife. The party of five then rode on quickly through several villages just stirring to life in the cold dawn. Annie and the men looked for a secluded spot to change into Tibetan dress. At the top of the next mountain pass they stopped and the Englishwoman slipped on a dark red Tibetan robe rather like a voluminous dressing gown girdled at the waist with a wide sash. Then, at last, they were ready: Annie Taylor had decided the time was right to make her bold dash to the forbidden city of Lhasa.

Exactly twenty years earlier, when Nina Mazuchelli had taken an expedition into the Himalayas from India, she had been severely hampered by both the dress of her day and the current attitudes toward women. Annie, by contrast, could adopt any dress, mingle with any class of people, and travel unchaperoned anywhere. She

Annie Taylor in Tibetan dress.

too was English and a single woman traveling among men, but she was also a Christian missionary; and society approved of anyone engaged in Christian works.

For eight years Annie had waited on the edge of Tibet, in India to the south and China to the north, watching for just a crack in the closed door that she might slip through to carry the message of Jesus to the heathen heart of the forbidden land. While it was true that she did not reach Lhasa, she came closer to it than any European traveler since the famous French Jesuits, Abbés Huc and Gabet in 1846.[1] And she was the first European woman to enter Tibet proper.[2]

Her astonishing journey excited the Christian missionary world. Victorians doted on daring explorers and Miss Taylor qualified as a minor celebrity for the brief period she was in England after her Tibetan journey. She was asked to speak to geographical as well as evangelical societies even though she had made no scientific observations whatsoever. She mentioned a primula or two and the herds of wild animals but she scarcely noticed the terrain and was indifferent to geography. Yet her journey was described as "epoch-making for Tibet," and she was enthusiastically compared in some missionary books and magazines to Dr. David Livingstone, the great missionary-explorer. Livingstone had made careful surveys of all the ground he covered and kept daily records in his diary of barometric pressure, temperature and rainfall. Annie's diary was the barest record of her daily progress. What she lacked was an adequate education; what she had was initiative, imagination, and unbounded courage.

One characteristic Annie Taylor and Dr. Livingstone did share was that both were first of all servants of God: their restless spirits were sustained by unquestioned faith in the will of God and His Grand Design, in which they merely served as His instruments. Because their convictions were typical of the Victorian period it was not surprising that Annie's admirers overlooked her scientific shortcomings. One wrote: "As Livingstone by his great journeys opened the way for the Gospel into dark Africa, so our sister expects that God will use her journey to pave the road for missionaries in Tibet."[3] Enough people agreed with Annie for her to form "The Tibetan Pioneer Band" and lead them back to Asia.

By her own account, Annie had been fired with missionary zeal at an early age. When she was sixteen and a boarder at Clarence House School, Richmond, she was taken with her classmates to hear a stirring lecture given by John Moffat, the son of Dr. Moffat, a great African missionary and the father-in-law of Livingstone. But Mr. Moffat's inspiring account of brave and dedicated workers spreading the Gospel in distant, uncivilized lands was directed only to the young men in his audience. He discouraged missionary work for women, describing in graphic terms the hardship encountered abroad, and concluding that women were only a hindrance to the men in their important work. For the first time in her life, Annie remembered, she fervently wished she were a boy.

She was at an impressionable age, a girl not attracted to the social role expected of a young lady from a well-to-do family: she refused to dance, to attend the theater, or ride out on Sundays. But she was highly susceptible to the romance of travel and adventure, which was not surprising considering her family background. "All Taylors," she wrote when she was older, "are born travelers with an interest more than usually keen in what is strange and remote." Her father, John Taylor, was a director of the well-known Black Ball Steamship Line, a Fellow of the Royal Geographical Society, and a constant international traveler. Her mother, of French Huguenot descent, was born in Brazil, and their home was frequented by friends of Mr. Taylor from all over the world.

Ann Royle was born into this peripatetic family at Egremont, Cheshire, on October 17, 1856, the second oldest of ten children. She was so frail she was not expected to live. Her childhood was plagued by chronic bronchitis and a "valvular disease of the heart," according to William Carey, a highly respected English missionary, who knew her.[4] Her schooling was scant and irregular. As a semi-invalid she was no doubt indulged, for she developed a wilfulness that hardened as she grew older into a stubborn determination to have her own way.

Annie's early life was related with her approval by Isabel Robson in *Two Lady Missionaries in Tibet*.[5] Robson said when Annie was thirteen years old she knelt down after one Sunday evening service and dedicated herself to a life of Christian work, an ideal she pursued single-mindedly through her entire life. At eighteen, she and her two younger sisters were sent to school in Berlin, but Annie soon became ill and returned to her parents' home in Brighton. Here she began to visit the sick and continued her charitable work. When her family moved to London she extended her visits to the poorest sections of the city. Recalling those youthful days she wrote, "I have found in the slums exactly as I have since found in my Asiatic journeys, a woman is rarely molested if she makes it quite clear that she is doing her duty quietly and unassumingly."

But Annie's father viewed her occupation with displeasure. Tensions mounted between them until he, at last losing his patience, ordered her back to her social and home duties. Annie refused. Now twenty-eight years old, she sold her jewels to take cheap lodgings in Marylebone and to pay her fees for an elementary medical course, including midwifery, at nearby Queen Charlotte's Hospital. The same year she learned that "the Lord wanted women for China," a recognition of the worth of her sex in the evangelical field overseas that she had longed for. Annie applied and was accepted as a missionary by the China Inland Mission.

Happily, Annie's mother had felt "the comforts of Christ" in a little chapel in Sicily, where she had spent the winter, and finally understood her daughter's consuming passion to serve the Lord. Mrs. Taylor returned to London, urged a reconciliation, and Mr. Taylor conceded to the extent of paying for Annie's passage to China and providing her with the necessary outfit. But he stopped her allowance as an indication that he was not giving his wholehearted sanction to her venture, and with a certain amount of scepticism regarding her staying power, gave her letters of authorization to several steamship lines for a return passage home.

Annie sailed from England on September 24, 1884, and arrived in Shanghai about eight weeks later. At first she stayed with a

Mr. and Mrs. Judd at the Mission's post in Chinkaing not far from Shanghai, in the estuary of the Yangtze River. Presumably she plunged into mission life without any delaying cultural shock. She attended emotion-charged services heavy with exhortations and heartfelt hymn-singing similar to those she knew at home. But she also had to learn the Chinese language and customs to be able to live as close as possible to the people. It was a tenet of the China Inland Mission that its workers minimize the barriers between them and the Chinese by adopting Chinese dress and manners. Within seven months, by May 1885, Annie was sufficiently prepared to be posted farther upstream on the Yangtze. She wrote from An'ching, "Miss Barclay and I are now very happily settled with dear Miss Matthewson at the West Gate House"—three missionary women in a strange and sometimes hostile country trying, through free medical advice and simple home remedies, to win the friendship of the Chinese so they would listen to the Gospel teachings.

Since the late 1870's the China Inland Mission had sent unmarried women alone into interior China. Sometimes they were the sole Westerner in inland cities and districts. It was a period when China's xenophobia was being challenged by the West, and the Manchu dynasty under the dowager Empress reluctantly permitted a few foreigners to travel from their footholds in the port cities to the interior. The Protestant missionaries were among the first to push far inland; often they were the first contacts the Chinese had with Westerners.[6] Their sudden appearance in an ancient and unchanging culture inevitably aroused suspicions. "Everywhere the missionary is jealously watched," one Mission chronicler wrote, "and at any moment his work may be stopped by official interference or popular resistance."[7]

The command "to go into all the world and preach the Gospel to every creature" was the motivating force of evangelical missionaries. As itinerant preachers they measured their success not so much by converts (in 1890 there were only about 50,000 Protestant Chinese in China) as by the number of cards, with translations in the native tongue of Gospel messages, handed out in the belief that once the Word was received, the power of its truth would triumph. Sowers more than cultivators, they tirelessly sought fresh fields to give what *The Times* called, "the gift which is itself good, and the giving of which is perfect."[8]

To hold steady against resistance or hostility and to keep one's purpose clearly in mind were essential for a missionary in China. Annie had those qualities. In 1887 she was sent to Lanchou, the capital of Kansu, China's westernmost province, an area then known as Chinese or Outer Tibet, bordered on the north by the Great Wall and on the south by Tibet proper. There is no record of Annie's imagination being excited by her surroundings although she traveled alone among Tibetan encampments for the first time. To her Lanchou was simply "a wicked city." She wrote a short article for *China's Millions,* the Mission magazine, titled "The Degradation of Women." The July 30, 1887 issue of the magazine reported that on one journey alone in Kansu Annie distributed 1,300 Tibetan text cards.

Fairs were ideal places to reach great numbers of people so Annie traveled west from Lanchou, about a week's journey by horseback, to the great Tibetan Buddhist monastery, Kumbum. Kumbum ranked third among monasteries of importance to Tibetans, and was an ancient seat of learning, housing more than 3,000 monks. Here Tibetans gathered every year for a religious festival and great fair. Annie was one of the first Europeans to visit this Central Asian monastery, which is to this day isolated and mysterious, remote from any modern route of travel.[9]

Annie went to the Kumbum fair in 1887 armed with only her faith and a sheaf of Tibetan text cards to present to the undoubtedly astonished lamas. She made a handful of notes about her visit, later transcribed by William Carey.[10] Thanks to his effort it is known that Annie stayed at an inn that she considered "very dirty." Her room, she wrote, "was one of a row of little pigeon-boxes built on the roof, which is slanted. It has no furniture in it but a brick bed, my rights to which were disputed by its small in-habitants. We made a fire of brushwood on the roof, as we had to do our own cooking."

But Annie was impressed by the gold-roofed monastery, its red-robed lamas and the great Tibetan camp of white tents on the surrounding hills. Fond of homey comparisons, she wrote that these white tents pitched in the wilds of Central Asia "were like those we are accustomed to see in England." Herds of cattle, horses, yaks, and camels grazed around the camp and in the valley was a row of fair stalls set up by Chinese merchants.

Once settled, Annie climbed to the encampment. The Tibetans "would often run away when I approached," she said, "and one man nearly struck me when I offered a text card to his little wife. They thought at first that I was a man, because my ears were not pierced. But soon I made friends, and then they would invite me to sit in the midst of them on the hillside. Some came to see me in the inn."

Annie liked the Tibetans. The houses of the lamas she found "scrupulously clean whereas the Chinese are dreadfully dirty." Of course she knew they lived in spiritual darkness and she decided "the lamas are not at all intellectual looking; they go about telling their beads, with a little dog." But they were "a religious people," and she did not blame them for their ignorance: "Poor things, they know no better; no one has ever told them of Jesus."

Physically the Tibetans appeared to her "a muscular, well-built race," and "the men seem fond of their wives, taking their hands and making them walk in front. They laugh and talk together —so different from the Chinese. . . . In the evenings," Annie recounted, the Tibetans "had drinking bouts, in which the women joined; they sat in a ring on the hill and sang songs. . . . Drinking is one of the evil habits the civilized Chinese have taught the Tibetans." Still, she did not condemn them for that either. Their open, cheerful manner matched hers and she was easy among them.

Altogether the simple, semi-nomadic Tibetans seem to have appealed to Annie more than the settled Chinese. Her contemporaries claimed that she had read about Tibet when she was a girl and the faraway, mysterious land "laid hold of her mind" at that time. It was a romantic notion Annie did not deny, but chance, rather than a conscious plan, seems to have brought her in contact with the Tibetans. More likely it dawned on her slowly round the campfires at Kumbum that she might be the first to bring the Word to interior Tibet—an irresistable thought.

A "dear old Tibetan man" sold her two wooden bowls for three-pence and showed her his stock of provisions done up in leather bags. In her usual matter-of-fact manner she observed that "six little loaves of bread, each as large as an English halfpenny roll, cost a penny; milk was three farthings a quart." Perhaps with an eye to the future she noted that "a Mohammedan who is friendly with the Tibetans told me he could get me a small house in a Tibetan village for ten pence a month." Some Tibetan women visited her at the inn and tasted her tea and cakes. (She was a skillful cook according to Mr. Carey, who claimed her family teased her by saying it was her *one* talent.) In return the women then invited Annie to visit the Kumbum temples with them. Unlike later travelers, who described the great gilded Buddhas, the rich display of brightly painted banners, the altars crowded with brass basins of holy water and lighted butter lamps, the pungent smell of burning incense and the clamor of long Tibetan trumpets and leather drums, Annie simply took quick notes and observed critically: "The people bowed down before the images, but behind the door were some lamas drinking tea and enjoying themselves," and "visitors put cash on the table in front of the idols." In the monastery Annie was asked by a Tibetan woman to look at her child's badly burned arm. The arm was covered with blisters and plastered with fresh cow dung. Annie cleaned and dressed it with linseed oil and flour. "The mother was very grateful," she reported, "and I think I got a little nearer the hearts of the Tibetans and lamas who were looking on." In a letter to the director of the China Inland Mission, Annie wrote there was a great need for mission work among the Tibetans, dutifully stating, "If no one else is found to go among them, *I must*"; but she told a contemporary that "after studying Chinese for five years, her spirit failed her at the thought of acquiring a new language."

The year after her visit to Kumbum Annie became ill with consumption (probably tuberculosis) and had to return to the coast.

On her way downriver she survived the sinking of her boat at the Han rapids when the boatmen, reeling from a night of drinking, smashed against the rocks. Her parents telegraphed her to join them in Australia where they were traveling. She did, and after a short recuperation went on to visit her married sister in Darjeeling, India (apparently with the Mission's approval, for *China's Millions* reported, "Miss Annie Taylor sailed on Thursday, September 5, 1889, in the P & O *Khedive* for Calcutta, en route for Darjeeling to work among the Tibetans in the neighborhood while learning more of their language").

Once in Darjeeling Annie found a native hut to settle in at nearby Ghum, where she could associate with Tibetans. In March 1890 she moved across the British–Indian border to the Sachen Valley in Sikkim, only to be promptly ordered out by the Sikkimese authorities. She stayed her ground and the captain of the guard from the Chinese fort at Khamba-jong came down to settle the trouble. Annie managed to secure permission to lodge in a room at the monastery but the people were forbidden to sell her food. In this untenable situation Annie nearly starved. She picked up grains of corn spilled from the caravans passing through the village, had fever, and was asked by the Sikkimese what she wished done with her body when she died. "I have always found," she had once stated, "that persons who set out for the mission field in the expectation that they are going to the death usually do die. For my part I have always believed that I shall live as long as God has work for me to do." Her frail constitution was sustained by this resolute spirit.

Before she left Sikkim Annie gave some medical treatment to a youth from Lhasa named Pontso, about nineteen years old, who had run away because of the cruel treatment he received from his master in Tibet. Gratitude decided him to become Annie's servant and a Christian convert. There was a feudal quality in Pontso's attachment to Annie: he was willing to share her fortunes, good or bad. It was the kind of arrangement many Westerners in Asia seemed to have no uneasiness accepting. For the next twenty years Pontso traveled with Annie in China, Tibet, India and England.

One evening in March, 1891, Annie was writing letters home from Darjeeling, when suddenly, she said later, a voice commanded her to "go to China." As if to underline the order, the evening's post brought the sailing dates of the China Mail from Calcutta. So off Annie went, Pontso with her, on the next ship for Shanghai. Although missionary friends warned them that Pontso quite likely would be beheaded if he returned to Tibet, the two proceeded to the interior of China and took up residence at Tauchau, on the Tibetan border in the province of Kansu, where no Englishwoman had been before. There they worked and waited a year before making their headlong dash into Tibet.[11]

Never in the annals of Tibetan exploration could there have been so naive and ill-prepared an attempt to reach Lhasa as Annie's. Well-financed, extensively equipped and armed expeditions led by experienced, travel-hardened men had preceded her and failed. Yet this small woman, a semi-invalid in childhood, now thirty-six years old and still highly susceptible to pulmonary diseases, was determined to make her way over mountain passes and across the barren, wind-swept plateau of Tibet proper.

The average elevation of the Tibetan plauteau is 15,000 feet. Year round the morning temperature stands at about $-18°$ Centigrade ($0°$ Fahrenheit) and can rise to $38°$ Centigrade ($100°$ Fahrenheit) at noon. It was a country where banditry was one of the chief occupations and foreigners were prohibited on penalty of their lives. Annie had only the vaguest notion of the obstacles ahead of her.

She knew there were three high roads from the Chinese border to the capital of Lhasa. Once she was safely past the border checks, Annie planned to take the Sining Road that originated in the Kansu province. It passed for the most part through uninhabited country and water was scarce. If a traveler could make it to Kegu, the half-way stop between the Chinese border and Lhasa, he could exchange tired horses for fresh mules or yaks. From Kegu to Lhasa there were occasional encampments of Tibetans who sometimes were willing to sell meat or tea.

Tauchau, the old Chinese city where Annie made secret

arrangements for her journey, was a center for trade with Tibet. Caravans formed outside the city walls, then wound their way up the hills and over three passes, each with gates guarded by Chinese soldiers who collected customs and watched for interlopers. The little caravan Annie managed to take through these three gates consisted of herself and five Asians: Noga, her Chinese guide and head servant, returning to Lhasa with Erminie, his Tibetan wife; Pontso, Annie's faithful Tibetan servant; and two other young men, Leucotze and Nobgy. They had six pack horses and ten mounts. Nina Mazuchelli's far less ambitious expedition employed seventy men. In contrast to Nina's extensive traveling paraphernalia, Annie carried two tents, bedding, cloth for barter, presents for chiefs and food for two months. Her personal kit consisted of two tin basins, a wooden bowl or two, a copper pan, together with a knife, fork and spoon. But shortly after crossing the border, Annie's party was attacked by Tibetan robbers and relieved of most of their belongings. Annie lost all of her extra clothes, her camp bed and bedding and two horses. Nogby, one of the young men, lost heart as well, and turned back to China. Six weeks later the other, Leucotze, died of the cold on a snowy pass. "He was a big, strong-looking man," Annie said, and added: "The Master has called to account the strong, and left the weak to go on and claim Tibet in his name."

Noga, the third Chinese, turned out to be a wife-beater, thief and liar, who was afraid he would be killed by the Tibetans for bringing an Englishwoman into Tibet. He quarreled with Annie, his wife, and everyone else. One night after Annie had gone to bed, Erminie came to her tent. She was "in tears," Annie wrote, "her husband having been thumping her; and in a little while he followed with his horsewhip. I told her to get behind my bed, and then seized hold of the whip, and screamed, which frightened him. Pontso with his blanket wrapped around him tried to hold him; but being so little a man and Noga so tall, it was not much use." But Annie held him off with the whip. Later in the trip, he threw a copper pan at Annie and reached for his sword; a Tibetan merchant chief intervened to save her. Noga then went ahead to Lhasa and

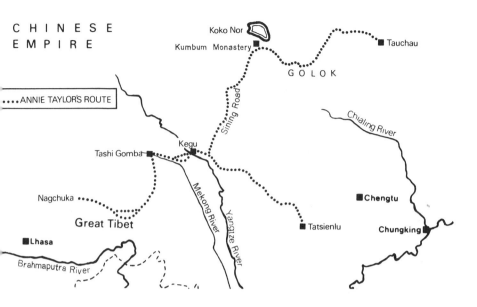

CHINESE
EMPIRE

Koko Nor

Kumbum Monastery

Tauchau

GOLOK

...ANNIE TAYLOR'S ROUTE

Sining Road

Chialing River

Tashi Gomba

Kegu

Mekong River

Yangtze River

Nagchuka

Great Tibet

Chengtu

Lhasa

Tatsienlu

Chungking

Brahmaputra River

abandoned the trip. Annie and Pontso hid for two days in a cave, relieved at his departure even though they knew he was going to tell officials she was nearing the capital.

With all the calamities Annie would experience—robbed of all her possessions, all but two of her horses dead or stolen, and she so weak she could not walk—the thought that she might not live seems never to have occurred to her. For twenty nights she slept out in the open—in a hole if she could find one to protect herself from the icy winds; a cave became a luxury. When she could not find a caravan to travel with she often followed bands of wild horses through the snow, trusting their sure-footedness to save her from falling into crevasses. Wolves howled at night. In the day the snow glare burned her eyes and made her ill. On October 8 she jotted in her diary, "Have two men to escort us. . . . One is a lama, but he is also a hatter, for he made my foxskin cap for me. They are both big, fine men. The snow is on the ground, and it is very cold, a piercing wind." By October 23 she was so weak she nearly fell off her horse. Pontso "mixed sal-volatile and brandy" and she went on. November 5 she wrote, "over another pass. We had just descended when my little white pony lay down under me, quite done up." November 20: "I have got so thin and am so exhausted that it looks as if I could not go on without a good horse. God will provide one for me. Pontso has been crying today. We expect to start tomorrow."

The next day in the encampment where she had stopped, a Tibetan chief let her have a good horse in place of two of her bad ones, "for he pitied me, as I am not strong enough to walk." Annie traveled for a few days with the caravan and reported that the same chief "who is with us takes great care of me, getting his men to give me hot water for tea, and making a fire for me to warm by. It is such a treat after the way I have been treated by Noga." The Tibetans gave her butter and cheese. A terse entry in Annie's diary for December 18 read: "It snowed. Very cold. I am getting used to sleeping in the open air." She was traveling alone now except for Pontso and Penting, another Tibetan who had joined her. On December 20 she wrote, "I made two puddings of some suet that I begged, a few currants, some black sugar, and a little flour. One is to be for Christmas day. The cold is extreme." On December 24 she found an old camp site above the road where there was grass and plenty of yak dung to build a fire with. December 25 Annie reported: "We are resting in our pleasant hiding place. A nice Christmas Day, the sun shining brightly. I had fellowship in spirit with friends all over the world. Quite safe here with Jesus." She prepared tea and put her Christmas pudding on to boil. After two hours it still was not warm in the middle, and she was moved to comment that "This is a strange climate." She ladled the boiling tea out of the pan with wooden bowls, but if it were not drunk at once it was covered with ice.

A few days later Annie cut off her hair "as all *annis* do." *Anni* is the Tibetan word for nun, a nice play on Annie's name; Tibetans always called her Anni. But her disguise was minimal; she wore Tibetan dress and spoke the language.

When she was arrested on January 3, 1893, just three days' march from Lhasa, there was no doubt Annie was English. Weak and exhausted as she was, she conducted herself with all the dignity, determination and sheer courage her countrymen justly pride themselves on. Annie's own account of the incident, shortened slightly from her diary, best conveys her cool manner under extreme duress.

"January 3.—Passed a very cold night. Soon after starting we saw men with guns and horses. Noga had told their chief that an English woman was coming along, and they had orders to stop us. They said we must halt by a stream that was near till the chief came up. We all sat down and made tea. Pontso and Penting fear much for their lives. May God save them! Our hope is in him, and he will do it. After tea the two men were relieved by others, and in the evening their chief arrived. . . . He was very affable, but he kept guard over us all night with his men. There were five of them all together, armed with guns and swords. The two who first met us have been sent to Nag-chu-ka to give information of our capture to the civil officer or principal chief.

"January 4.—This morning we were taken to a place where there was better grass for the horses. It was a ride of only half an hour.

"Our meat and butter are all gone, and tea and barley-flour without butter are difficult to digest.

"The Nag-chu-ka chief is expected on the sixth. The wind is cold. A caravan from Lhasa encamped near us this evening. A lot of people came to have a look at me.

"January 5.—A military chief has arrived with a band of soldiers. He came in the early morning, and after pitching his tent, called for Pontso and asked him many questions.

"The chief was courteous, but declared we must go back the way we had come. I had an interview with him, and said this was impossible, that we had no food, that our horses were done up, and that I could not stand the severe cold. I had been brought into these straits by Noga, who had taken two of my horses and had tried to kill me. He had promised we should be in Lhasa in two months, but already four had elapsed. I must see the Nag-chu-ka magistrate, and lay my case before him. To return simply meant to die on the road."

Eventually the chief relented and sent for an official from the little town of Nag-chu-ka. Two days later he arrived. Annie felt he was very rude when he questioned her. "I told him I must have courtesy," she said. "If there were chiefs, surely there must be justice; and I must have justice." She insisted on seeing the principal chief. "I had to be very firm, as our lives seemed to rest on my taking a firm stand."

Annie persisted and the official gave in, agreeing to let her plead her case to a higher authority. The military chief who had captured her detailed an escort of thirty soldiers to take her and her two servants to his encampment, about a day's ride away. "I felt truly proud of my country," Annie said, "when it took so many to keep one woman from running away."

Annie waited at this camp for three days. On January 11 she wrote, "The wind is so strong that it blows the tent down. I washed my sleeves, so as to look a little respectable tomorrow when the big chief arrives." On January 13 she spent much of the night in prayer, and she wrote the next day: "In the morning the people were all busy putting up tents. They told us that the big chief was coming. About midday he arrived, followed by Noga and his wife. Pontso and Penting are much afraid. The chief called for Pontso to speak with Noga about the things I said he had stolen. I sent word that a servant could not speak for his master and that I must go myself.

"He invited me to come. I went, and a mat was placed for me to sit on. The principal chief and the second one, a lama, were both sitting in state.

"He asked many questions, and wanted to know why I had come to their country within three days of Lhasa.

"I said that I wished to cross it to get to Darjeeling.

"He said that the Tibetans were at strife with the English, and that the war question was not settled, also that Noga denied having any of my things, except the horses, which he alleged I had given him.

"I said that I had not. . . . Noga was then called in, and denied having anything of mine. . . . I had never heard such lying.

"They said they would send soldiers and escort me out of Tibet.

"I said, 'I am English, and do not fear for my life.'

"They said they would send Noga and me back to China.

"I said they might carry my corpse, but they would not take me against my will.

"The chief favored Noga's side rather than mine. He said that Noga was Chinese, and I English, and so he could do nothing for me. . . . I said: 'Is this Tibetan justice? Noga has done a great wrong to me; you say you cannot punish him. To harm me personally you fear. . . . You want to send me on the road with horses that cannot go, and without a tent, knowing that in a few days we shall have to stop in a place swarming with brigands; and thus seek to be rid of me, not killing me yourself, but getting me killed by others. I can only say that if you do not help me to return I must stay where I am. . . .

"The chief then spoke quite civilly, and said they did not quite know what to do."

Clearly the Tibetan chief had never dealt with anyone at all like Annie. She was fearless and demanding. A captive with no weapon except pride, she negotiated and won from the chief a promise of an escort and horses, blankets and food for her return trip. Then she complained that the sheepskin he sent her was not good, the butter rancid and the horses unfit: "I never in my life saw such a collection of skeletons. I said that they were worse than mine, and would have none of them."

On January 18, two weeks after her capture, Annie was sent back over the road of ice and snow on which she had struggled for four and a half months toward Lhasa. The Tibetan chief gave her an escort of ten soldiers to accompany her for eleven days. Then she and her two men were on their own again.

Annie's return trip to Tatsienlu, the tea center in Szechwan, on the Tibetan border, took her from January 18 until April 13, 1893. In her diary she briefly understated this journey of incredible hardship. Typical entries were: "March 17.—Started before sunrise. It was bitterly cold. I got nearly frozen, and was very glad when the sun came up. My horse gave out. We hoped to have cleared the pass, but had to stop on this side. Snow very deep. Slept on the snow. "March 18.—Could not sleep for the cold. Crossed the Mo Ra La, the worst pass I have had. One of the horses was frozen to death going over. We saw the remains of two yaks and a horse which had dropped on the way. The sun was so bright that we were in danger of sunstroke and of freezing to death on the selfsame day. The men had bad eyes. They protected themselves by putting their hair over their eyes."

The last entries in Annie's small diary were: "April 13.— Arrived at Ta-chien-la. Found some French missionaries who were very kind. They took me to a good inn kept by a Tibetan woman whose husband is a merchant. "April 15.—Left for Kiating and the coast."

All told, she had traveled about 1,300 miles in seven months and ten days. It was astonishing that she returned alive.

It seems that Annie had no intention of writing a book about her perilous journey. Yet the high adventure of it motivated her to keep an almost daily record, written with frozen fingers when she was faint with hunger and exhaustion. When William Carey visited Annie in 1899 at Yatung on the Sikkim-Tibet border, she used the diary to answer some of his questions. But she could scarcely read it any more; some parts could not be made out at all. Later he asked if he might transcribe it. "In due time it arrived," Mr. Carey wrote, "very odoriferous of Tibet, being packed with butter, foxskins and goatskins, dried mutton, yaks' tails and jo." He soon saw it would be a slow and serious task deciphering those already half-obliterated hieroglyphics. However, by patiently poring over each of the 162 closely written pages with a magnifying glass he managed to transcribe it. Carey "pruned" the diary and edited it for "slips of grammar, and crude forms of expression," so it is impossible to know how much of the essential Annie Taylor was edited out by him.[12] Could she, after living eight years in Asia at a very primitive level of society, make observations and self-revealing comments Mr. Carey might not have deemed seemly for a Victorian lady? There is no way to know. Carey was scrupulous

Annie with the Tibetan Pioneer Band.

enough to state that Annie in her naïveté had lent her name to exaggerated claims that she was the first European in Tibet, and he rectified that erroneous impression by giving the public Annie's diary, "in its wholeness and its simplicity . . . fresh, original impressions penciled down on the spot."

So even some of the documents in Annie's name are not really hers. Her character was filtered through Carey's sensibilities and an idealized image promoted by her colleagues and family. No chinks in her Christian armor reveal more than a single-minded woman supported in her self-made way of life by an unshakeable faith in God—and ultimately by an inheritance. As Annie stated it, "God has in His goodness given me sufficient means (some eighty pounds a year), through deceased relatives, to fully supply all my own requirements."

On returning to England, Annie left the China Inland Mission and formed her own missionary group, the Tibetan Pioneer Mission. It was a presumptious name that irritated even some of Annie's supporters since it seemed to ignore the work of other missionaries (particularly the Moravians and Roman Catholics) among the

Tibetans in India and China. The origin of the Mission, as reported in *The Christian,* was "Miss Annie R. Taylor's journey into Tibet proper, in the course of which she proved the possibility of gaining an entrance for the Gospel into [Tibet], that country so long believed to be closed to the emissaries of Christ. . . ."

Annie was in great demand to speak. In December of 1893 she described what she had seen of Tibet to the Royal Scottish Geographical Society meeting in Edinburgh. At missionary meetings in England and Scotland she made appeals for workers and shortly had sufficient response to choose nine men to form The Tibetan Pioneer Band, dedicated "to live and die for Tibet." One man had a wife and child whom she welcomed, but she did not call for women as she felt, herself excepted, they were not up to the hardships of Tibet. On February 16, 1894, a farewell meeting for the Band was held at Albert Hall, London. Annie related her journey once again to an enthusiastic audience. But within a few months of the Pioneer Band's arrival in India and their ill-planned move to Sikkim, differences cropped up between Annie and her workers. She asked to be relieved of her responsibilities and suggested the men join the China Inland Mission, which most did.

Like nearly all adventurers Annie was essentially a loner, intent on her own way, mesmerized by her own vision and impatient with others. "Looking back on my life," she said, "I see that I have seldom undertaken what everybody else was doing. I have always preferred to strike out a new road and then, when the way was made tolerably smooth, I have left it for others to travel. In this sense I may consider myself a pioneer."

Stubbornly determined to find a way back to Tibet, Annie, with Pontso, stayed on in Sikkim at Gangtok, on the tea road to India. In the evenings when the Tibetans camped with their caravans on the mountainside, Annie would join them as she had done in China at the Kumbum fair—a small Englishwoman in Tibetan dress, sitting crosslegged round a campfire in a circle of Tibetans. "I have given away nearly 3,000 text cards," she wrote home from Gangtok. But seeing no way to slip into Tibet, she moved north over the 14,000-foot Jelep Pass to Yatung on the border between Sikkim and Tibet. The Tibetans allowed the British to keep a trading station at Yatung and for permission to reside there Annie had to become a trader. Her sister Susette visited Annie at Yatung and wrote accounts of her trip for a London newspaper, *The Guardian,* in 1903.[13]

"Quite low down in the valley," Susette wrote, "while threading my way through the pink pine stems of a wood, I suddenly became aware of an advancing figure that exactly suits the surroundings. A brick-red gown of native cloth, with a glimpse of fawn silk at neck and wrists and pouched up above the girdle, thus displaying blue cloth trousers tucked into fur boots the shape of nightsocks, drapes a small person with a merry face, much too fair for a native, and topped by a yellow peaked cap. It is my sister! She greets me affectionately, asks if I have had a pleasant journey— much as if she were meeting me at Victoria Station—and takes me to the Mission House which has been her home since 1895."

The Mission House was built of rough pine planks, the shingles of its roof weighted down with stones, "Yet when we pass through the tiny kitchen into the parlor," Annie's sister said, "there is an attempt at real cosiness." The ceiling was papered with the *Weekly Times,* "hard to beat for solidity." The walls were draped with Indian calico, white flowers on dark red. There was a bit of carpet, a round table covered with books, a large brass samovar in the corner, a stove, two folding armchairs and stools. A wall clock, some pictures, pink primulas in a little deal window-box and small flower pots all round the room completed the picture. In another building Annie had her general store, selling to the Tibetans "cloth and calico, vinegar and sweets, the wares and ornaments of China and Japan."

When the Younghusband Expedition, the British military force on its way to Lhasa to settle rights of trade and access with the Tibetans, passed through the Chumbi Valley they established a camp. Annie, now forty-seven years old, offered her services and was appointed a Nursing Sister in the field hospital. She took off her red Tibetan robe, packed away the yellow one given her as a mark of honor by the lamas, and put on English clothes again. As

Yale

Annie with Pontso and Sigju.

soon as she moved to her small house at the camp she planted
flowers in front of it. According to her sister, Annie got on well
with the soldier "because she has a strong sense of humor, and
appreciates his peculiar form of wit."

Pontso and his new wife, Sigju, were left in charge of the
trading post at Yatung. Sympathetic to both sides in the British–
Tibetan conflict, Annie was heartbroken that its conclusion did not
open Tibet to traders and missionaries, but only increased the
Tibetans' hostility to foreigners. And unauthorized travel into the
country Annie had set her heart on evangelizing was now more
impossible than ever. No longer fortified by her dream, Annie's
health declined. She returned to England sometime after another

sister and brother-in-law visited her in 1907. Nothing more is known of her—not even the date of her death.

But Annie's epitaph could have been borrowed from Livingstone's: Her "life was spent in an unwearied effort to evangelize the native races." Eccentric, ill-educated, Annie had responded to the irresistable lure of a forbidden land. In her bold dash into Tibet she symbolized all those unknown Victorian women whose craving for adventure found an approved outlet in the service of their churches that sent them—wives and unmarried women in the hundreds—traveling alone to the far reaches of the Empire, and sometimes beyond.

'Tis not too late to seek a newer world
. . . for my purpose holds
To sail beyond the sunset, and the baths
Of all the western stars, until I die.

Tennyson
Ulysses

ISABELLA BIRD BISHOP (1831-1904)

"I HAVE ONLY ONE formidable rival in Isabella's heart," said her husband, Dr. Bishop, "and that is the high tableland of Central Asia."[1] He understood that Isabella Bird's greatest passion was travel. She had made extensive journeys far off the usual globe-trotters' routes in North America, the Hawaiian Islands and the Orient before she consented, late in life, to become Mrs. Bishop. And the more she traveled the more Central Asia, especially Tibet, attracted her. Twice she rode to the edge of Tibet proper, once from India and once from China. Both times she stopped short of a reckless plunge into the wild interior. A Victorian lady who was trained for Christian duty and service, Isabella tried to keep her exuberant romanticism checked, her amazing energy channeled into acceptable activities, and her restless temperament controlled. In the process she developed two distinctly different personalities: the invalid lady and the robust traveler.

Even though she was beset with physical ailments that would have left most Victorian women of her class languishing on plush sofas, Isabella made heroic journeys by boat, train, mule, pony, yak,

Isabella Bird Bishop, from the frontispiece to one of her books.

elephant and sedan chair. She wrote nine travel books—all best-sellers. And she was the first woman elected to the prestigious male preserve of the Royal Geographical Society. In the late 1800's, that great period of intelligent and articulate travelers, Isabella Bird Bishop was the most famous of a redoubtable band of British lady travelers. However much these women tried to disguise their motives with treatises on botany, the uplifting effect of the natural landscape, the quaint customs of the natives or the need for the civilizing influences of Christianity, they were at heart explorers and adventurers. And diminutive Isabella was the most intrepid of them all.

Isabella Lucy Bird was born October 15, 1831, at Bourough-bridge Hall, Yorkshire, the first of two daughters in an upper-middle-class family with a long tradition of devotion to good causes. It was a sternly religious but loving family that Isabella remembered, with her clergyman father the central influence. She was a sickly child and doctors ordered that she spend as much time as possible out-of-doors. So her father propped her on the saddle in front of him until she was able to ride her own horse beside him as he made his parish calls. Together they observed the countryside. Anna Stoddart, Isabella's devoted friend and first biographer, quoted her recollection of those happy days riding with her father in Cheshire, where they moved when she was three years old: "he made me tell him about the crops in such and such fields, whether a water-wheel were under-shot, or over-shot, how each gate we passed through was hung, about animals seen and parishioners met." He taught her to measure distance with her eye, to read the signs of the seasons, to know the proper names of flowers and trees. Isabella was an apt and eager pupil. "Her brain was never stunted by rebuff," said Mrs. Stoddart, "nor stultified by baby language."[2] She was taught the Bible straight, not diluted in a children's version, and she was expected to remain standing through the long Sunday services. From this early training Isabella developed a formidable endurance, learned to take in great blocks of information and observe everything carefully and accurately, and she became an expert horsewoman.

In 1842, when Isabella was eleven, the family moved to Birmingham (largely because of her father's quarrel with the Cheshire cheesemakers who refused to observe the Sabbath). When she was older Isabella helped teach in his Sunday school. At sixteen her fervent nature found an odd outlet in an invective she wrote against free trade and in favor of protection. The essay was privately published, presumably by her family. Writing was always her most satisfying form of expression.

Through childhood and adolescence, Isabella's health continued to deteriorate. At the age of eighteen she had to undergo surgery to remove a fibrous tumor from her spine, and when she did not measurably improve, her doctors prescribed that Victorian panacea—travel. In July 1854, Isabella sailed from Liverpool to visit her cousin stationed at Prince Edward's Island, Canada. Provided with £100 from her father and a blessing to stay as long as it lasted, Isabella seemed to make a startling recovery. She traveled west—by steamer, train, and stagecoach over pot-holed roads—to Quebec and Montreal, Chicago and Cincinnati, and back through New England. Completely on her own for the first time, she blossomed. All her long and sprightly letters home were saved by her family and when she returned her father urged her to put them into book form. With a completed manuscript in hand she confided to an author she met that she was looking for a publisher; he read her work and was sufficiently impressed to forward it to the distinguished London publishing house of John Murray. Isabella was only twenty-five years old when Mr. John Murray the third, who was to become her life-long friend and mentor, published her book: *The Englishwoman in America*. This vivacious travel book, which enjoyed a considerable success, was full of Isabella's descriptions and observations—all remarkably assured for a girl of twenty-three. She contrasted the condition of American women to her own and it is clear she would not have changed places:

However fond they may be of admiration as girls after their early marriages they become dutiful wives, and affectionate, devoted mothers. And in a country where there are few faithful attached servants, the more devolves upon the mother than English ladies have any idea of. Those amusements which would withdraw her from home must be abandoned; however fond she may be of traveling, she must abide in the nursery; and all those little attentions which in England are turned over to the nurse must be performed by herself, or with her superintending eye. She must be the nurse of her children alike by day and by night, in sickness and in health; and with the attention which American ladies pay to their husbands, their married life is by no means an idle one. Under these circumstances, the early fading of their bloom is not to be wondered at, and I cannot but admire the manner in which many of them cheerfully conform to years of anxiety and comparative seclusion, after the homage and gaiety which seemed their natural atmosphere in their early youth.

Isabella's own milieu was highly social and she enjoyed it. Her trip to America was one great whirl of introductions from one family to the next. Home again, her health declined as it always did when she attempted to settle into a lady's life. Her younger sister Henrietta was, like their mother, temperamentally more suited for the quiet routine of receiving visitors in the sitting room, calling on the sick and needy and attending lengthy Sunday services. Isabella must have been pleased that her doctor prescribed another trip to America. This time she stayed nearly a year. Her father suggested that she investigate the much-talked-about religious revival in America, and from Maine to Kentucky to Iowa she "listened to no fewer than one hundred and thirty sermons, some of them preached to Indians, to trappers, to negroes and by negroes." Shortly after Isabella returned to England in 1858, her father, "the mainspring and object" of her life, died. In accordance with his wishes, she wrote *The Aspects of Religion in the United States of America,* published in 1859.

With her mother and Henrietta, Isabella moved north to Edinburgh. During the next few years she was so ill from her spinal condition that, as Mrs. Stoddart records, "she could seldom rise before noon; but all her correspondence was done in the morning, as well as many of her numerous articles for *The Leisure Hour, The Family Treasury, Good Words,* and *Sunday at Home.* She wrote propped up by pillows, a flat writing-board upon her knees, and letters or sheets of manuscript scattered around her."[3]

In 1866 Mrs. Bird died and the sisters, Isabella and Hennie, settled into the affectionate, dependent relationship that sustained them both until Hennie's death fourteen years later. Hennie tended the hearth and the wandering Isabella wrote letters home. Eventually Hennie settled in Tobermory, a picturesque seaside village in the Inner Hebrides Islands off the west coast of Scotland. There in The Cottage, overlooking the harbor, Hennie would sit by the window and read Isabella's marvelous letters to friends and admirers. In spite of having to wear a steel net to support her head when she sat up, Isabella managed to travel through the highlands and the Outer Hebrides, and to work vigorously for a scheme to help the poorer residents of the West Highlands emigrate to Canada.

Lady Middleton, one of Isabella's many friends from that period, wrote that even then she "was a very extraordinary woman. Her quiet, slow, deliberate manner of speech might have been a little tedious in one less gifted; but when the measured sentences at last came forth, you felt they had been worth waiting for. She had very projecting upper teeth then, and they may have affected her utterance, but she had the pluck to have them replaced."[4]

Isabella continued still to be plagued by bad health. In addition to her spinal trouble she now suffered from insomnia and periods of deep depression. Doctors could not cure her, nor did a conventional cruise to New York lift her from her slough of despair. So this time a prolonged stay in sea and mountain air was ordered. On July 11, 1868, Isabella left Edinburgh for Australia and New Zealand. She was thirty-seven years old, depressed and very ill.

Australia seemed uninteresting and New Zealand unbearably hot and dusty: "she was appalled by the drunkenness everywhere," said Mrs. Stoddart. In Auckland she boarded the *Nevada,* a ship bound for the Sandwich Islands. The *Nevada* was a government-condemned old paddlesteamer. It was listing and taking in water; its mainmast was sprung, several of its boiler tubes burst and its starboard shaft was partially fractured. Two days out of Auckland the *Nevada* encountered a South Sea hurricane. The wind howled. Heavy seas struck the old steamer so she groaned and strained and nearly split asunder. The storm raged for more than twelve hours: death by drowning was a distinct possibility. And suddenly the small, sick spinster from Edinburgh was aroused and tingling with life. "At last I am in love," she wrote home to Hennie. "And the old sea-god has so stolen my heart and penetrated my soul that hereafter, though I must be elsewhere in body, I shall be with him in spirit. . . . To me it is like living in a new world, so free, so fresh, so vital, so careless, so unfettered, so full of interest that one grudges being asleep; . . . no thoughts of the morrow . . . keep one awake . . . no vain attempts to overtake all one knows one should do. Above all, no nervousness, and no conventionalities, no dressing. It sounds a hideously selfish life. . . ."

At this juncture Isabella realized she could manage her life on her own terms as long as she was away from home. She could indulge her passion to commune with nature on tempestuous seas and in rugged mountains. The stimuli she needed to satisfy her insatiable curiosity were out in a wider world, not in the cultured but restricted circle of her Edinburgh friends. From now on she was committed to travel. To the end of her days she made retribution for not staying home and doing the good works expected of her. Whenever she returned home she gave to charitable causes, lectured to church groups and the Y.W.C.A., made soup and carried it to the sick. She established a "Shelter and Coffee Room" for cabmen in Edinburgh. Much later she founded a missionary hospital in memory of her husband in Kashmir, another for Hennie in Pakistan, and three more in China. But despite her guilt she clung to the freedom she found while sailing through the South Seas to the Sandwich Islands.

The Hawaiian archipelago was well off the beaten track at that time. Isabella was surprised to see the Hawaiian women riding astride their horses like the men. She tried it and discovered to her delight that is was infinitely more comfortable than a sidesaddle. Immediately she had a riding costume made out of MacGregor plaid. "I am beginning to hope I am not too old, as I feared I was, to learn a new mode of riding," she wrote Hennie. "I wish you could see me in my Rob Roy riding dress." She galloped about the exotic landscape, climbed to a volcano's rim, and had such an exhilarating time it was difficult for her to leave for the United States en route home.

From San Francisco Isabella took a train to Truckee, California, in the Sierra Nevada and hired a horse to ride into Lake Tahoe—a venture nearly cut short when she was offered any one of "three velvet-covered sidesaddles almost without horns." After her Hawaiian experience of riding astride, "I felt abashed," she said. "I could not ride any distance in the conventional mode and was just going to give up," when a man told her that in Truckee she could ride as she wished. Under her long dust coat Isabella had on her Rob Roy riding costume. "In no time a large grey horse was 'rigged out' in a handsome silver-bossed Mexican saddle. I strapped my silk skirt on the saddle, deposited my cloak in the corn-bin and was safely on the horse's back before his owner had time to devise any way of mounting me."

Isabella rode off to see for herself what life was like in the mining camps and pioneer settlements of the Wild West. "Once on horseback my embarrassment disappeared," she noted. From September to mid-December she traveled alone through California and Colorado. At ranches and mining camps she helped with the cleaning and cooking. She learned to drive a wagon and to round up cattle. And in the Colorado Rocky Mountains she probably fell in love. The man was Jim Nugent, a Plains scout known as "Mountain Jim." In a letter to Hennie, Isabella described him as "a man for whom there is not now room. . . . Ruffian as he looks, the first word he speaks— to a lady, at least—places him on a level with educated gentlemen, and his conversation is brilliant, and full of the light and fitfulness of genius." He was a man of about forty-five, who "must have been strikingly handsome. Tawny hair, in thin uncared-for curls, fell from under his hunter's cap and over his collar. One eye was entirely gone."

Clearly, Isabella was captivated. She and Mountain Jim rode in Estes Park and climbed Long's Peak, where Jim lifted and dragged her the last 500 feet to the 14,700-foot summit. "As we were leaping from rock to rock," Isabella wrote, "Jim said, 'I was thinking in the night about your traveling alone, and wondering where you carried your derringer, for I could see no signs of it.' On my telling him that I traveled unarmed, he could hardly believe it, and adjured me to get a revolver at once."

In the clear air of the Rockies, Isabella felt supremely fit and up to anything. Pat Barr, Isabella's later biographer who had access to all of her letters, says the encounter with Mountain Jim was the first time her "whole nature was aroused." Her instincts for warmth and compassion had been developed but her latent sexuality was primly repressed. In an unpublished letter quoted by Ms. Barr, Isabella confided to Hennie a dream that would lend itself to a Freudian interpretation—an interpretation that undoubtedly would have deeply offended Isabella. "I dreamt last night," she wrote, "that as we were sitting by the fire Mr. Nugent came in with his revolver in his hand and shot me. . . ."[5]

In his vain and dashing manner Jim pursued Isabella; emotions ran high. But Jim drank and had ugly moods. Isabella's practical nature triumphed over her romanticism and she concluded that he was, for all his charm and undeveloped talent, "a most painful spectacle." Reluctant to leave but emotionally exhausted, she returned with some relief to familiar, devoted Hennie, "my own darling." Six months later Jim was shot dead by the man on whose ranch Isabella had stayed for so many exciting weeks in the Rockies.

Back home Isabella worked furiously at her writing. In 1875, fourteen years after he had published her first book, John Murray brought out *Six Months in the Sandwich Islands,* an instant success. *A Lady's Life in the Rocky Mountains* followed four years later.

During this period in Edinburgh Isabella, full of Victorian eagerness for self-improvement, found time to enroll in a botany class. There she met Dr. John Bishop, a physician ten years her junior. He was a gentle, sympathetic man, much admired by his patients and colleagues, who had come from Sheffield to Edinburgh to establish a private practice. As a former assistant to Sir Joseph Lister and a resident surgeon at the Royal Infirmary, his credentials were impeccable. Anna Stoddart reported that "he was an ardent microscopist, and Miss Bird and he were busy with the marvels of the Atlantic ooze."[6] He was captivated first by Isabella's intellectual ability and then he fell in love with her.

Dr. Bishop had none of Jim Nugent's boldness or Isabella's restlessness. He was one of those solid, reassuring people so comforting to anyone torn by anxiety and indecision. Very soon he became Hennie's and Isabella's doctor. In 1877 he made his first proposal of marriage to Isabella. But she, now in her mid-forties, held him off with the plea that she was not "a marrying woman." Mrs. Stoddart reported that she "persuaded him to let their friendship abide undisturbed by considerations which she was unwilling to face."[7] Isabella wrote that Dr. Bishop was noble and sweet about her refusal and "behaved beautifully." What she probably feared, Pat Barr speculates, "was the physical intrusion of sex, and even more, the curtailment it would have imposed upon her freedom of action, especially while she was of child-bearing age." Ms. Barr is certain that Isabella, though normally sexed, simply directed her passion "in channels other than sexual," and concludes, "she had no maternal instincts whatsoever, preferring, in the legendary British fashion, the company of horses."[8]

Whatever the reason, Isabella avoided John Bishop's attentions by leaving Edinburgh. Early in 1878 she was off across America again, this time to Japan, where she shunned the conventional traveler's sights and struck out for the Japanese hinterlands. Turning south to Singapore, Isabella heard about a ship leaving for Malaya. Impulsively she decided to book passage on it. She had reached her full stride as a world traveler—adaptable and equal to any opportunity.

While in Malaya she must have thought about Hennie—sitting on a windowseat in The Cottage, or tending to her garden above the quiet village—and known the expression on her sister's face when she read a passage that excited or amused her. Isabella had a decided gift for character delineation and small drama.

"Yesterday," she wrote from Taipeng, "when a tall, slender, aristocratic-looking man, who scarcely looks severable from the doorsteps of a Pall Mall club, strode down the room and addressed me abruptly with the words: 'The sooner you go away again the better; there's nothing to see, nothing to do, and nothing to learn,' I was naturally very much interested."

Proud as she was to be British and confident of the superiority of the British way of life, she sometimes encountered colonials she thoroughly disapproved of. "Mr. Bloomfield Douglas, the Resident [at Klang], a tall, vigorous, elderly man, with white hair, a florid complexion, and a strong voice heard everywhere in authoritarian tones," was one. His residency was an armed camp. Isabella spent the night there and "when the moonlight glinted two or three times on the bayonet of the sentry, which I could see from my bed, I thought it was a Malay going to murder the Resident, against whom I fear there may be many a *vendatta*."

Upcountry she rode an elephant and reported: "This mode of riding is not comfortable." But she enjoyed crossing a river on its back, when "the elphant gently dropped down and was entirely submerged, moving majestically along, with not a bit of his huge bulk visible, the end of his proboscis far ahead, writhing and coiling like a water snake every now and then, the nostrils always in sight, but having no apparent connection with the creature to which they belonged." She was sitting in the water, "but it was nearly as warm as the air," and so she went, "some distance up the clear, shining river with the tropic sun blazing down upon it."

In the heart of the jungle she stopped at the British Residency at Kwala Kangsa, but Mr. Low, the Resident, was away. As far as Isabella could determine she was the only European in the entire region. It was a bizarre situation—the type that Isabella always found enormously appealing. She wrote Hennie:

I was received by a magnificent Oriental butler, and after I had a delicious bath, dinner, or what Assam was

"The author's first ride in Perak"—an illustration from THE GOLDEN CHERSONESE.

pleased to call breakfast was served. The word "served" was strictly applicable, for linen, china, crystal, flowers, cooking, were all alike exquisite . . . a smart Malay lad helps him, and a Chinaman sits on the steps and pulls the punkah. All things were harmonious, the glorious coco-palms, the bright green slopes, the sunset gold on the lake-like river, the ranges of forest-covered mountains etherealizing in the purple light, the swarthy faces and scarlet uniforms of the Sikh guard, and rich and luscious odors, floated in on balmy airs. . . .

My valise had not arrived, and I had been obliged to dress myself in my mud-splashed tweed dress, therefore I was much annoyed to find the table set for three, and I hung about unwillingly in the verandah, fully expecting two Government clerks in faultless evening dress to appear, and I was vexed to think that my dream of solitude was not to be realized, when Assam more emphatically assured me that the meal was "served," and I sat down, much mystified, at the well-appointed table, when he led in a large ape, and the Malay servant brought in a small one, and a Sikh brought a large retriever and tied him to my chair! This was all done with the most profound solemnity. The circle being then complete, dinner proceeded with great stateliness. The apes had their curry, chutney, pineapple, eggs, and bananas on porcelain plates, and so had I. The chief difference was that, whereas I waited to be helped, the big ape was impolite enough occasionally to snatch something from a dish as the butler passed round the table, and that the small one before very long migrated from his chair to the table, and sitting by my plate, helped himself daintily from it.

That night "tigers came very near the house, roaring discontentedly . . . I have now been for three nights the sole inhabitant of this bungalow!" Isabella reported. "I have taken five meals in the society of apes only. . . . Dullness is out of the question."

Mr. Low, a bachelor, returned and asked Isabella to stay on another month at Kwala Kangsa. "You've the pluck of six ordinary men," he told her, "and you glide about the house and never speak at the wrong time."

But Isabella felt she must not linger; she had to hurry home to Hennie. In Cairo she caught a fever, and was a "wreck" when she landed in England. "My body is very weak," she wrote a friend from Tobermory, "and I can only walk about three hundred yards with a stick; but my head is all right, and I am working five hours a day in this delicious quiet." She was writing *The Golden Chersonese* about her Malayan experiences. It was her last book based on letters to her beloved sister.

In April, 1881, Hennie contracted typhoid fever. Dr. Bishop moved into The Cottage to care for her, but early in June she died. Isabella was disconsolate. Dr. Bishop pressed his offer of marriage and the next year, with Isabella still in mourning, they were married. She was fifty years old and John Bishop forty. Perhaps she accepted the kind, devoted doctor as a replacement for her sister. Mrs. Stoddart contended that had Hennie lived, Isabella never would have married. In any event, her married life was short. During it she was ill most of the time and had another spinal operation. Dr. Bishop developed pernicious anemia and Isabella tended him with loving devotion until he died in 1886, just a few days short of their fifth wedding anniversary.

Now Isabella was without anyone to make a home for her. Having no talent for domesticity herself, she floated from one lodging to another, trying to settle on a way of life. At Tobermory she gave French lessons and drawing lessons on alternate days—and shocked the local folk by tramping about and rowing across the bay dressed in a man's ulster, a weather-beaten old hat, and big snow boots. Early in 1887 she went to London to take a three-month course in nursing at St. Mary's Hospital, Paddington. Next she decided to care for invalids in a house she leased in Maida Vale, London, but it became "unendurable." Mrs. Stoddart perceived that "unrest had seized upon her, and she mistook its fever for the misery of solitude."[9]

She quarreled with the Anglican church she had been reared in and was baptized by total immersion but did not join the Baptist sect. Finally she hit upon an acceptable rationale for travel: she would go to Asia to establish missionary hospitals in memory of her sister and husband.

Missionary life had never attracted Isabella, and she was sometimes critical of it; but the more she traveled in the East, the more she became convinced that Christianity was the only hope for improving the lives of the great mass of exploited, ignorant people. "How corrupt is Buddhism," she declared. Everywhere she was horrified by the oppression of women, especially under Islam. Later, when she traveled in Persia, her abhorrence of the Muslim seclusion of women and the practice of polygamy was deepened by her experiences. "These false faiths degrade women," she asserted. "The intellect is dwarfed, while all the worst passions of human nature are stimulated and developed in a fearful degree: jealousy,

Isabella in Manchu dress.

envy, murderous hate, intrigue running to such an extent that, in some countries, I have hardly ever been in a woman's house, or near a woman's tent, without being asked for drugs with which to disfigure the favorite wife, to take away her life, or to take away the life of the favorite wife's infant son."

But Isabella herself did not feel personally oppressed enough to have any sympathy with the woman's suffrage movement. Social and political change at home did not interest her. Amelioration of existing conditions through the establishment of hospitals abroad (she gave the money and left the organizing to someone else) was as close to social action as Isabella cared to come. She did rather relish one brief excursion into politics when she published two articles in *The Contemporary Review* of 1891, on "The Shadow of the Kurd." These led to an invitation to speak in a Committee Room of the House of Commons, and to be questioned closely at a dinner party by the great statesman, Mr. Gladstone, on what was called "The Armenian Question."

Her two latest books, *Unbeaten Tracks in Japan* (two volumes), 1880, and *The Golden Chersonese*, 1883, sold briskly, and she was financially quite secure. But Hennie was no longer waiting anxiously for her wonderful tales and Isabella, in her fifty-eighth year, felt that this next voyage to the East would be "a strange time, a silent interval between the familiar life which lies behind . . . and the strange unknown life which lies before." She was reading all she could on Persia and India and Sir Edwin Arnold secured for her a bluebook on Tibet. Her plans were taking shape. "I wish you could see my outfit," she wrote to a friend, "packed in four small boxes, 20 in. long, 12 in. wide, and 12 in. high, a brown waterproof bag containing a canvas stretcher-bed, a cork mattress, blankets, woolen sheets, a saddle, etc."

The saddle—Mexican, of course, with a horn—she soon had on the back of "a beautiful creature, Badakshani bred, of Arab blood, a silver grey." Isabella had gone via the Suez, "that blazing ditch," and arrived in Karachi March 21, 1889. She proceeded to Lahore and Islamabad, then on to Srinagar in Kashmir. But, she complained, "there was no mountain, valley, or plateau, however

remote, free from the clatter of English voices and the trained servility of Hindu servants, and even Sonamarg, at an altitude of 8,000 feet and rough of access, had capitulated to lawn-tennis. To a traveler, this Anglo-Indian hubbub was intolerable," and she left Srinagar on June 20 "for the uplifted plateaux of Lesser Tibet."

Isabella's party consisted of herself and four men: a Punjabi bearer and interpreter, a groom, a coolie, and an Afgan soldier from the Maharaja of Kashmir's irregular force of foreign mercenaries. The Maharaja had sent the soldier, Usman Shah, to escort Isabella when she entered Kashmir. "This man," she wrote, "was a stage ruffian in appearance. He wore a turban of prodigious height ornamented with poppies or birds' feathers, loved fantastic colors and ceaseless change of raiment, walked in front of me carrying a big sword over his shoulder, plundered and beat the people, terrified the women, and was eventually recognized at Leh, as a murderer"—after Isabella had traveled with him for nearly a month deep into the Himalayas. Still, she was somewhat charmed by his swashbuckling manner and was sketching him in full costume with sword at his side when soldiers swooped down to arrest him.

"An attendant of this kind is a mistake," she concluded, not because she felt he posed any threat to her but because he terrorized the villagers. This made things difficult. She had to purchase supplies at the small infrequent villages she passed through. Always a light traveler, Isabella carried for food only tea, dried soup and a little saccharin.

In Isabella's estimation the best member of her party was Gyalpo, her horse. "He was higher in the scale of intellect than any horse of my acquaintance," she wrote. "His cleverness at times suggested reasoning power, and his mischievousness a sense of humor. He walked five miles an hour, jumped like a deer, climbed like a *yak*, was strong and steady in perilous fords, tireless, hardy, hungry, frolicked along ledges of precipices and over crevassed glaciers, was absolutely fearless, and his slender legs and the use he made of them were the marvel of all. He was an enigma to the end . . . quite untamable. . . ." In a letter to Lady Middleton, Isabella admitted Gyalpo was "not an old woman's horse, but I contrive to get on with him."

Isabella's destination was Leh, the capital of Ladakh, a small Himalayan dependency of Kashmir in Little Tibet. To get there she had to cross three mountain passes, "like three great steps from Kashmir to the Tibetan heights," she explained. The first pass, the Zoji La, had an elevation of 11,578 feet. The track was a rough, narrow switchback cut from a sheer wall of rock. In places it was made up of broken ledges, some four and five feet high, up which the horses had to leap and scramble. As she climbed Isabella found the air "exhilarating," and experienced a wonderful sense of "daily-increasing energy and vitality." Now a widow nearing sixty, she was in her element and at last finding her feet again. At the summit she beheld an entirely different landscape: treeless mountains of bar gravel and rock, with snow-crested summits and deep, snow-filled ravines. "It was," she wrote in her book *Among the Tibetans*, "CENTRAL ASIA."

Gyalpo was as high-spirited as his unlikely rider: "the clever, plucky fellow frolicked over the snow, smelt and leapt crevasses which were too wide to be stepped over, put his forelegs together and slid down slopes like a Swiss mule, and though carried off his feet by the fierce surges of the Dras [river], struggled gamely to shore." Isabella was completely in control of herself, her lively horse, and her little band of untried men. She recorded the daily routine of her journey: up at six, she sent the coolie ahead with a small tent and a lunch basket to await her half-way; then she started off at seven with Usman Shah (the murderer) ahead of her, leaving the other two servants to follow with the camp. Halfway in the day's ride she halted to rest in the small tent for two hours. At the end of the march a simple "afternoon tea" was followed two hours later by a dinner of boiled rice and roast meat—bed by eight p.m. At the village of Shergol, her men managed to pitch her tent on a steep slope and had to place her trestle bed astride an irrigation channel. Here she met her first Tibetans. The headman came down to meet her and showed her through the small monastery built into the rock. It was painted blue, red, and yellow, and one of the representations of the deities she thought, bore "a striking resemblance to Mr. Gladstone."

When Isabella arrived in Leh, the little capital of flat-roofed, many-balconied houses high up in the Ladakh range of the Himalayas, great caravans were arriving daily from Kashmir en route to all parts of Central Asia. The colorful bazaar, bustling with Lhasa traders and merchants from Amritsar, Kabul and Bokhara, delighted her. But she gave no intimation of a longing to follow the ancient caravan route any farther across the desolate Tibetan plateau. A lone dash to Lhasa, like Annie Taylor's from the Chinese border, was not her style. Instead, as so often happened with Isabella, she fell in with an interesting male traveling companion. In Leh she met Mr. Redslob, a German Moravian missionary who was very knowledgeable about the Tibetans, spoke their language, and was much admired by them. He was "a man of noble physique and intellect, a scholar and linguist, an expert botanist and an admirable artist," she said, so when he proposed a three-weeks journey to Nubra, "a district formed of the combined valleys of the Shayok and Nubra rivers, tributaries of the Indus, and bounding in interest . . . of course I at once accepted an offer so full of advantages." (The Nubra Valley is bounded on the north by the great Karakoram mountain range where Fanny Bullock Workman and her husband explored a few years later.) Accompanied by the energetic missionary, Isabella scrambled up rocky crags and poked into Tibetan monasteries all across the Nubra. She examined the prayer wheels and listened to the monks chanting, studied the frescoes, looked at sacred volumes of "exquisite calligraphy on parchment," and heard the dissonant clash of cymbals, horns and thundering six-foot drums. "It was not music, but it was sublime." To Lady Middleton she wrote, "I like the Tibetans *very much*."

She rode a yak "with an uncertain temper," which "usually made a lunge at one with his horns . . . It was a new thing for a European lady to travel in Nubra," she said, and the people "took a friendly interest in my getting through all right." For Isabella "getting through" was riding on a yak over a 17,930-foot summit with snow falling, then down a steep ascent of 3,500 feet "where under a cloudless sky the mercury stood at 90°!"

The water was dangerously high at the ford of the Shayok river which Isabella and Mr. Redslob had to cross to return to Leh. Against her better judgment Isabella was persuaded to cross on a big Yarkand horse instead of her "spider-legged" Gyalpo. The water was deep and almost ice-cold; the current was so strong "the horses simply seemed treading the water backwards." For half an hour they struggled against the current. Finally Isabella's horse made a desperate effort to leap the bank, "but fell short and rolled over backwards into the Shayok," with Isabella under him. "A struggle," she wrote, "a moment of suffocation, and I was extricated by strong arms [Mr. Redslob's?], to be knocked down again by the rush of the water, to be again dragged up and hauled and hoisted up the crumbling bank. I escaped with a broken rib and some severe bruises, but the horse was drowned. Mr. Redslob, who had thought that my life could not be saved, and the Tibetans were so distressed by the accident that I made very light of it, and only took one day of rest."

Back on Gyalpo, she rode up to the monastery of Deskyid, "the most imposing in Nubra." As Gyalpo "pluckily leapt up the great slippery rock ledges . . . the Tibetans cheered and shouted 'Shabaz!' (well done!)."

Leaving Mr. Redslob at Leh, Isabella made a detour to the encampment of a nomadic tribe of Tibetans called the Champas, in the Rupshu country, an arid plateau at a 13,500-foot elevation in southeast Ladakh. She engaged two muleteers with four horses and two yaks loaded with twelve days' hay and barley for Gyalpo. At one difficult ford Isabella's men balked. She roped them to her and "in this compact mass we stood the strong rush of the river safely." She crossed the Togland Pass at a height of 18,150 feet and descended to the caravan camping ground. "News travels as if by magic in desert places," Isabella commented. By evening there was a wild rush of Tibetan horsemen around her. "The headman dismounted, threw himself on his face, kissed my hand, vaulted into the saddle, and then led a swirl of his tribesmen at a gallop in ever-narrowing circles round me till they subsided into the decorum of an escort." When they reached a river near the camp, "Two men took my bridle, and two more proceeded to put their hands on my stirrups; but Gyalpo kicked them to the right and left amidst shrieks of laughter, after which, with frantic gesticulations and yells of 'Kabardar!' I was led through the river in triumph and hauled off my horse. The tribesmen were much excited. Some dashed about, performing feats of horsemanship; others brought apricots and doughballs made with apricot oil, or rushed to the tents, returning with rugs; some cleared the camping-ground of stones and raised a stone platform, and a flock of goats, exquisitely white from the daily swims across the river, were brought to be milked." Isabella was invited to visit each of the forty-odd tents.

Traveling on she met sheep caravans of up to 7,000 sheep,

each animal with a packsaddle loaded with twenty-five to thirty-two pounds of salt or borax from Tibet proper. "On three nights I camped beside their caravans, and walked round their orderly lines of sheep and their neat walls of saddlebags; and far from showing any discourtesy or rude curiosity, they held down their fierce dogs . . . and not one of the many articles which my servants were in the habit of leaving outside the tents was on any occasion abstracted."

After she left the Tibetan camp Isabella entered a region of barren rock and gigantic mountains. She crossed great waterless stretches where there was not a tree or animal in sight. One night she picked a campsite beside a glacier-blue river she guessed was near the boundary of British Tibet. Suddenly a Tibetan appeared as if from nowhere, followed by a man in nondescript dress. But across his chest was a band with the British crown on it. "I never felt so extinguished," Isabella moaned. "Liberty seemed lost, and the romance of the desert to have died out in one moment!"

She returned to Leh via the Lahul valley, then took five weeks making her descent from Little Tibet in the Himalayas. She journeyed through the Upper Kulu Valley and the native states of Mandi, Sukket, Bilaspur, and Bhaghat. Early in November, completely refreshed, she reached Simla.

However far she was from the supporting authority of civilization, Isabella never had any difficulties with her servants that she could not handle. Her rare gift for commanding respect and inspiring devotion seemed to be based on a firm belief in her own competency that she conveyed to others. At the same time she was equally clear about her expectation of the best in whomever she engaged. When the soldiers in Leh arrested her escort, Usman Shah, she was asked to inspect her baggage for theft but refused. "I had trusted him," she said, "he had been faithful in his way, and later I found that nothing was missing."

There must have been a certain magnetism about this unusual woman. Dorothy Middleton, the British writer, stated that "Isabella Bird was not everyone's favorite, inspiring in about equal proportions admiration and that kind of idolatry which women of vigorous personality command from their less strong-minded sisters."[10] But strong-minded men seemed to find her an attractive traveling companion. In Simla, where she had returned from Leh, she met Herbert Sawyer, a tall, handsome thirty-eight-year-old major in the British Indian Army. He was on his way to Persia on a military and geographical mission. Perhaps Major Sawyer felt this small, mature woman would be a good "front" for his expedition. In any event they shared an adventurous 500-mile ride from Baghdad to Teheran in mid-winter through some terrible blizzards —Isabella once was literally frozen to her saddle. Unprepossessing as her appearance was, she stood the test and Major Sawyer arranged to meet her later in southern Persia at Isfahan, where they set out to explore and survey the wild and barren country of the Bakhiari tribes. Pat Barr gives an account of the tension that eventually developed between them over "dealing with the natives."[11] Isabella was very upset at the Major's arrogant, imperialistic attitude. After they parted she rode on, alone, about 1,000 miles through West Persia and areas then known as Kurdistan and Armenia, to Trebzoid on the Black Sea where she took a steamer to Constantinople and from there reached London on Boxing Day, 1891. She had been away from England three years.

By now Isabella Bird Bishop was at the height of her fame. Dutifully she accepted a strenuous schedule of "missionary addresses," and tried to keep to her six-hour-a-day writing schedule. Within the year she brought out her two-volume *Journeys in Persia and Kurdistan*. It was received enthusiastically. "Persia is not an attractive country to write about," she told her publisher, John Murray. "The success is especially gratifying." Isabella had never been one to shy from the unattractive. Years before, this Mr. Murray's father had wanted the less experienced Isabella to excise from *The Golden Chersonese* her graphic descriptions of the jail she visited in Canton and of the Chinese use of torture. She refused. She always tried to give complete accounts of her travels, and the pious observations she interspersed on the benefits of Christianity were entirely in keeping with the assumptions of her period.

In 1892 she was elected a Fellow of the Royal Geographical

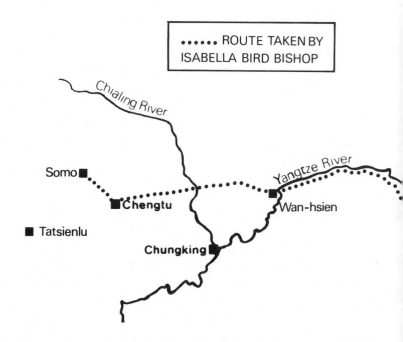

Society. She wrote Mr. Murray, "I am grateful for the innovation they have made in recognizing a woman's work." She was sixty-one years old. "I have become a very elderly—indeed I may say an old-- woman and stout! My hair will not turn grey and thus I am deprived of the softening and almost renovating influence which silver hair exercises on a plain face." Like her hair, her nature refused to change. Despite a medical diagnosis of "heart-failure" and rheumatic gout, she still could not resist the lure of the East.

From 1894 to 1897, from her sixty-third to her sixty-sixth year, Isabella traveled through Korea, Japan and China, and she made another journey to the edge of Tibet proper. On January 10, 1896, she left Shanghai by steamer and upstream changed to a houseboat, to ascend the Yangtze River for 300 miles. Disembark-

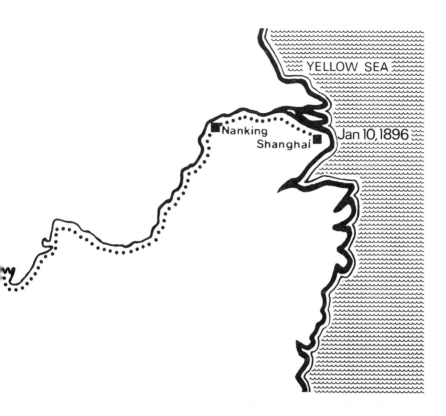

ing at Wan-hsien, she hired a sedan chair carried by coolies to transport her to Chengtu and back—with a detour to the Tibetan border—a trip of 900 miles overland that took three months. On several occasions she was attacked by Chinese mobs hostile to foreigners. Once she was struck unconscious by a rock that hit her on the head. That mob assailed her "with fiendish howls—a sound which once heard can never be forgotten," she declared.

But she would not be deterred from her plan to travel from Chengtu to Somo, a Tibetan mountain village on the West China border. Chinese officials, astonished at her audacity, tried to stop her. Messengers were sent ahead to order villagers not to give her transport or accommodation. The ever-resourceful Isabella related how, once she realized what was happening, she kept one such messenger behind her: "I jumped out of the chair, and set up my tripod [she had become a keen photographer] which he could not pass, and after a long attempt at the photography, baffled by the wind, told him and the others [her transport coolies] to keep behind, and not to leave me. The horseman kept trying to get in front, but as the path is very narrow and mostly on the edge of a precipice, I managed to dodge him the whole way by holding a large umbrella first on one side and then on the other!" In this improbable manner she reached the next village before the messenger.

The scenery on the way to Somo was wild and rugged. It reminded Isabella of Ladakh and the Nubra Valley in Little Tibet. In the dry, rarefied air of the mountains her umbrella split to pieces, her shoes cracked, screws fell out of her camera and her air-cushion collapsed. Her celluloid films became electric, emitting sparks when they were separated.

There was another terrible crossing of a pass in a snowstorm at night, when, she reported, "Several times I sank in drifts up to my throat, my soaked clothes frozen on me." She had fought through severe blizzards in the Zagros and Kurdistan mountains, but then it had been daylight. She had been on a good horse and had not been weakened by a wound from the rock that hit her head. Altogether, she decided, crossing the mountain pass to Somo was her worst experience. But the goal, as always, was worth it.

Isabella lingered in Somo for more than a week, energetically investigating the life of the Mantze people who lived there. She would have liked to go on to Ta-chien-lu, the great tea center to the south where Annie Taylor was sent on her expulsion from Tibet, and where later the Frenchwoman Alexandra David-Neel would live for several years. But this time official resistance and the news of tribal warfare along the route decided Isabella to retrace her steps. She had gazed at "CENTRAL ASIA" once again and savored old memories of her earlier journey to the edge of the unknown.

Korea and Her Neighbours (1898) and another two-volume book, *The Yangtze Valley and Beyond* (1899), recounted these last journeys. Isabella's stamina and fearlessness were a source of wonder to all the British diplomats and missionaries she stayed with. The comfortable assurance of age and success gave her the confidence now to wear what she wanted to cover her ample body. (Dr. Bishop had once wryly remarked, "She has the appetite of a tiger and the digestion of an ostrich.") One bachelor who was delighted to be her host in China described the costume she affected for travel, "which was designed to fulfill the Chinese canons of good taste."

The principal feature of it was a large, loose jacket, or mantle, of "pongee," which effectually disguised the figure of the wearer, but which unlike Chinese garments generally, was furnished with most capacious pockets, in which she carried all sorts of traveling paraphernalia, including some articles of her own design. Amongst other things, she used to produce from one of the pockets a portable oil lamp, ready for use at a moment's notice, and it seemed rather remarkable that the oil did not leak. If I remember rightly, she carried a loaded revolver in another pocket as a protection against robbers . . . yet there was nothing of that masculinity which is so common a feature in women who have made their mark in distinctively masculine fields of activity. Her manner was most sympathetic.[12]

In 1897 Isabella reluctantly left Asia for the last time. Her final days in London were a repetition of her earlier frenetic rushing about. She visited and received friends, lectured, wrote, and leased rooms at Kensington Crescent, London. Then she decided she wanted to be in the country and moved to Hartford Hurse near Huntingdon on the Ouse river, an hour and a quarter from the city. She began French conversation classes, lessons in photography and in cooking, and bought a tricycle to get more exercise.

In 1900 she closed up the beloved cottage at Tobermory in the Hebrides for the last time. "It is very odd," she mused, "to look at all things in the light of old age, and I am trying resolutely to face it, thankful all the time that my best-beloved never knew it and that they had neither to live nor die alone." She was trying to tidy up her affairs.

The next year, 1901, Queen Victoria died. She had come to the throne when Isabella was six years old and reigned for sixty-four years. Her death marked the end of an era and Isabella too felt her time running out.

Then in that year of national mourning the irrepressible Isabella Bird Bishop made a sudden, spectacular gesture of defiance against age and infirmity—a dramatic 1,000-mile ride through Morocco. It was an incredible last fling in her seventieth year—from Tangier to Marakkesh, and among the Berbers of the Atlas Mountains. She wished the Sultan of Morocco a long life and happiness, and he replied "that he hoped when his hair was as white as mine, he might have as much energy as I have! So I am not quite shelved yet!" she told a friend.

After her death in 1904 at the age of seventy-three, an article in the *Edinburgh Medical Journal* attempted to explain the paradox of Isabella Bishop.

It was difficult for it [the lay mind] to comprehend how a woman who in the quiet of her home life seemed so fragile, sensitive, and dependent could possibly submit to, or even survive, the experiences of her multitudinous travels. The Invalid at Home and the Samson Abroad do not form a very usual combination, yet in the case of the famous traveler these two ran in tandem for many years. Mrs. Bishop was indeed one of those subjects who are dependent to the last degree upon their environment to bring out their possibilities. . . . When she took the stage as a pioneer and traveler, she laughed at fatigue, she was indifferent to the terrors of danger, she was careless of what a day might bring forth in the matter of food; but stepping from the boards into the wings of life, she immediately became the invalid, the timorous, delicate, gentle-voiced woman that we associate with the Mrs. Bishop of Edinburgh.[13]

In 1960 the American historian Daniel J. Boorstin wrote an introduction to a new edition of *A Lady's Life in the Rocky Mountains* in which he said, "It is hard to recall another woman in any age or country who traveled as widely, who saw so much, and who left so perceptive a record of what she saw."[14] Isabella, guilty to the last about her traveling life, would no doubt be gratified to know that in the 1960's and 1970's almost all of her books have been republished with scholarly introductions attesting to their freshness, and to their lasting value.

"Those who are hardest hit by change are those who imagine that it never happened before"

Elizabeth Janeway
Man's World, Woman's Place

II. AMERICAN MOUNTAINEER EXPLORER:

FANNY BULLOCK WORKMAN (1859-1925)

WHILE WOMEN IN AMERICA were working to win the vote, New England-born Fanny Bullock Workman was climbing mountains and exploring glaciers in Asia. Fanny, a staunch feminist, regarded herself as positive proof that women could equal and even excel over men in the arduous life. She was a pioneer and wanted the world to know it. With her husband, Dr. William Hunter Workman, Mrs. Bullock Workman wrote eight thick books chronicling their adventures in Europe, North Africa, India and the ice-wilds of the great Karakoram and Himalayan mountain ranges.

A vigorous life was the antithesis of idealized femininity in the late 1800's. American women, like their English counterparts, were expected to lead circumspect lives. Most of them, conforming to this warped view of womanhood, were corseted and closeted, hampered by constant pregnancies and extended families, and burdened with the tedious trivia of Victorian manners. They were assumed to be too pure and delicate in thought and deed to respond to any physical challenge or competition. Fanny was unhampered by such restraining attitudes.

Fanny Bullock Workman.

Born into a wealthy Worcester, Massachusetts, family in 1859, Fanny was the second daughter and youngest of three children. Her father, a solidly respectable man, became Republican Governor of Massachusetts when she was seven years old. But some ancestral wanderlust may have passed to her from her great-grandfather, a sea-captain, and her grandfather, who was recorded to have felt an urge to travel in his youth (though he went no farther than from New York to Savannah before settling in New England to establish a family fortune based on trade and the manufacture of gunpowder). In this proper household Fanny was educated by private tutors. Then she was sent to Miss Graham's finishing school in New York and finally to Paris and Dresden for two years, where she became fluent in French and German, enabling her later to travel and lecture without the language barrier that separated most Americans from European life. In the spring of 1879 she returned home and in 1881, when she was twenty-two years old, married Dr. Workman, a prominent physician twelve years her senior. It was a most auspicious union. Dr. Workman was a graduate of Yale and Harvard and had traveled widely in Europe when he did postgraduate studies in Munich prior to his marriage.

The Workmans were an elegant couple, independently wealthy, with those composed countenances associated with the very rich. In scores of splendid photographs illustrating their books, William appeared straight-nosed and even-featured, perhaps rather grave and subdued, while Fanny's energy fairly radiated from her strong attractive face. Her large eyes were accentuated by thick arched eyebrows and her gaze was direct and penetrating. For her studio portraits she did her curly hair up bouffant style, then neatly pinned it back under her sun helmet for the road when William snapped her picture on their travels.

Early in their marriage William introduced Fanny to mountain climbing in the White Mountains of New Hampshire. She quickly became an enthusiast and scaled Mount Washington (6,293 feet) several times. In 1888 ill health obliged William to give up his medical practice, so he took Fanny and their daughter Rachel, who was four years old, to Europe. For the next nine years the

Workmans traveled with a vigor that would appal most robust men of today. With their headquarters mainly in Berlin, Munich and Dresden, and Rachel deposited in the care of a nurse or safely tucked away in a boarding school, they set out to do the Baedeker circuit. To their delight they discovered that they shared the same tastes in literature, art, and music (mainly Wagner). Relieved of the pressures he had as a practicing physician, William was getting to know his wife better than would have been possible had they stayed in Worcester. His most important discovery was that Fanny was as inspired by travel as he was. Years later William wrote—in their customary, rather stilted third-person nàrrative—that "From this point their lives and activities were inseparably united and they shared equally all the excitements, hardships, and the dangers of the adventurous life that followed, in meeting which Mrs. Workman was by no means the less courageous and determined."

In Europe the challenge of the Alps attracted the Workmans. There was considerable feeling against women climbers in the 1890's[1] but Fanny, with guides, ascended, among other peaks, the Zinal Rothorn (4,221 feet), the Matterhorn (14,780 feet) and Mont Blanc (15,781 feet). This unconventional life of travel and mountaineering suited Fanny's temperament. To continue in it she settled her domestic problems quite handily. By having no fixed address she eliminated household and social responsibilities. And to minimize family encumbrances she limited her progeny to Rachel, who in due time completed a proper English education at Cheltenham and London University. The great Victorian ideal was large families and information about birth control was not easily avilable, but William as a doctor must have had access to it.

Only in matters of dress did Fanny remain a conformist. Perhaps some ingrained self-image of great respectability made her eschew the sporting outfits of her day. Divided skirts, bloomers or Turkish-type trousers were not for her. For years she kept her ankles covered and wore her skirts so long they swept the dusty road. It was only well into the 1900's that at last she appeared in photographs with skirts high enough to reveal puttees at her shoe tops. She posed for William beside African mud huts, before

Indian caves and on temple ruins in long-sleeved white blouses trimmed by neat ties, floor-length skirts, a hat often with a veil and sometimes a striped parasol in hand. For climbing she wore full skirts that rose with the fashions showing her sturdy legs, eventually up to the mid-calf, encased in leggings.

Timed as if for Fanny's convenience, the stable safety bicycle appeared on the market in the 1880's. It had solid tires and no gears but was a great improvement over the cumbersome earlier models. By the nineties the bicycling craze had swept both Europe and America. With a sudden independence, thousands of women swept out of their musty Victorian parlors to wheel away un-chaperoned from their alarmed parents or husbands. Fanny, on her Rover Safety Bicycle, was ahead of them all.

With the newfangled Kodak equipment in her pack and a tin teakettle on her handlebars she and William wheeled down the Iberian Peninsula in 1895. The next year they pedaled across Morocco, over the Atlas Mountains and through Algeria. "A bright cold morning saw us in the saddle at 6:15," they wrote. Exhilarated by this new mode of travel and feeling a bit blasé about Europe, the Workmans decided to attempt a bicycle tour in Asia. In 1897 they sailed to Bombay. During the next three years they cycled from one end of the Indian subcontinent to the other, through Burma, across Ceylon and around Java.

Most men were fuming behind clouds of cigar smoke as they watched this "New Woman" which Fanny so magnificently personified wheel into the twentieth century. But not Dr. Workman. By now he and Fanny were launched on a new life as equals. And their marriage was strong enough to withstand even the strains of a writing collaboration. At intervals between their tours they would return to Munich or London to write their bicycling books with one voice. Together they wrote *Algerian Memories: A Bicycle Tour Over the Atlas Mountains to the Sahara* (1895); *Sketches Awheel in Modern Iberia* (1897); *Through Town and Jungle: Fourteen Thousand Miles Awheel Among the Temples and People of the Indian Plain* (1904).

William made a declaration of his sentiments in his dedication of *Modern Iberia*: "To my wife, my companion on long journeys awheel in most of the countries of Europe, in Sicily and North Africa, and on tours afoot in the mountains of Norway, the Alps, Apennines, Pyrenees, and Atlas, whose courage, endurance, and enthusiasm, often under circumstances of hardship and sometimes danger, have never failed, I affectionately dedicate my contribution to this volume."

And Fanny in the same book acknowledged her debt to William: "In memory of the varied experiences of our many travels together, I affectionately dedicate my portion of this book to my husband, without whose skill in planning the long route, energy in following it out, and attention to details, our journey through the length and breadth of Spain would not have been possible."

These bicycling books were well reviewed and had a wider audience than the five more factual mountaineering books that followed. They were written in a leisurely style and contained some appealingly romantic notions. In Spanish cathedrals, Fanny and William wrote, they were reminded of Wagner. At the Alhambra they lay on their backs to look up at the stone lions. In Algeria they rested "on grass sprinkled with violets, primroses and anemones" thinking how far they were from the gray brooding skies of Germany, here beside a babbling African brook watching the passing people "like a scene from the Arabian nights." Bicycling down a long desolate road over the Atlas Mountains they noted a lone shepherd "playing strange wild tunes on a reed pipe."

It was a carefree stimulating life, perhaps producing subtle changes in their characters, making it more difficult the farther they traveled from the centers of Western civilization to go back to the careful, routinized life in which they were reared. Some insidious alteration of their egos may have occurred, common to travelers, as if always being the observer gave one a superior insight untainted by commitment, a broader knowledge and sounder judgment than stay-at-homes or even travel experts. They registered severe criticism of the standard English *Murray Guides* and considered the French *Guide Joan* published by Hachette "the only reasonable guide of Algeria." Their *Modern Iberia* they stated, "was based

Fanny and William.

upon observations and experiences of the authors while on tour through Spain in the spring and summer of 1895." The tour was made on bicycles not to satisfy the spirit of adventure commonly ascribed to Americans, "but to present an intelligible portion of what may be seen in Spain today."

Pure pleasure in the pursuit of new experiences was an indulgence this New England couple could not allow themselves. Bred in their bones was the need to have clear goals and tangible evidence of their efforts. With sublime upper-class egocentricity they kept to their purposes. About their hostess at a Spanish *fonda*, they wrote, "an obese, oily-looking south Spanish woman met us on the landing, and as dinner would not be ready for half an hour, invited us into her private sitting room, where we found her husband and a friend. After a time, becoming weary of the conversation, we took out our notebooks and began writing our notes." The hostess' invitation smacked of a presumed social equality that may have bridled the Workmans. Like so many travel writers they saw foreigners as most attractive when there was a clearly understood distance between themselves and those they observed, and better still when the encounter underscored their own privileged worldly position as travelers. Feeling full of empathy, they recounted one Sunday morning when "The ladies all in black mantillas gathered around, asking us about our nationality and object in coming to Spain. As we went on they followed, and when we stopped a short distance farther on to take some views, they set their portable chairs, carried for church use, on the ground nearby, sat down and gave themselves up to the enjoyment of steady staring." Fanny and William were not irritated. They were inspired to speculate: "The long, intense, unblushing, yet respectful stare of the Spaniard must be another Moorish inheritance, it is so exactly that of the Arabs of the interior of Algeria and Morocco. A Spanish woman does not take a person in with a single, quick, penetrating, sweeping glance as does the English or American woman. She gazes steadily and in gazing does not seem to solve the riddle."

Fanny was sensitive and loyal to her sex; she never denigrated women less fortunate than she. The wistful, envious and hopeless looks her sisters gave her from Africa through Asia stirred her anger. "It is to be hoped," she wrote, "that light may fall upon the souls of men, that they may realize the great injustice practiced on the weaker sex, and that a day of awakening may come, when the latter may be free to develop as their nature demands." Everywhere she saw signs of their subservience. In an Algerian village, "We left the women and children in their desolate house with its floor of cold earth and returned to Salem's [the husband's] pleasant room with its carpeting of rugs, hoping in our hearts that if our Kabyle friend ever again should go to America, he would study the woman question." Even the memorial stones she and William found along the road in Gujerat, India provoked her sharp reaction: "One of the most complete stones found was a double one showing a man riding a horse on one side and on the other a woman's hand and arm, a touching tribute to the former position of women in India, the man carved trotting gaily through life, while the only scene pictured in that of the woman was her final sacrifice on the ashes of her lord."

However great her sympathy for her oppressed sisters, their submissiveness was not Fanny's style. She faced head-on her particular difficulties as a woman traveler. Savage dogs had attacked her on her bicycle in Switzerland and Italy, ripping at her skirts, so she and William acquired pistols and dog-whips. In Spain they had to draw their revolvers to stop a mule driver attacking them with a mattock. In Algeria packs of ferocious dogs were kept at bay by their steel corded whips. Once a somnolent hashish-smoking Moroccan led Fanny's mule into a slough, where it threw her. With her foot caught in the stirrup, she was dragged through the mud some distance before being rescued. It was scarcely the life for a gently educated lady—to follow unknown roads, to sleep in exotic accommodations, to eat irregularly and often badly. But it suited her. Pushing her loaded bicycle four hours at a stretch up a mountain pass, riding almost eighty miles in a day, forty-five of them uphill, powdered with the yellow dust from the plains of Castile, Fanny thrived.

Newspaper interviewers aware of the Workmans' fame sometimes plagued them. They pleaded ignorance of the language (untrue) to fend them off. One Spanish paper reported, "Señor Workman" and his *"esposa distinguida,"* arrived on two *"bicicletas magníficas,"* which they understood perfectly how to manage. By the time the Workmans went to India in 1897 for their three-year tour, Fanny was a seasoned traveler.

Ostensibly their 14,000-mile journey was to study the art, architecture and people of India. They had an impressive historical background, had read the great legendary Indian epics—the *Jakata,* the *Mahabarata* and the *Ramayana*—and were full of admiration for Hindu culture, particularly that which flourished before the despoiling Mohammedan conquerors, "when Europe was slumbering in the darkness of barbarism." They labeled the Taj Mahal "the most hackneyed sight in India," preferring the deserted red city of Fateh-pur-Sikri. Cognizant of the Hindu caste restrictions, they appreciated the problems for a Brahmin who, one terrible day when they were unable to find water, condescended to fill their teakettles. If the Brahmin should touch them or anything of theirs he would be defiled. "It is with a curious sensation," they declared, "that one accustomed by education to the feeling of superiority and pity, perhaps not unmingled with mild contempt usually entertained in Christian lands toward the unfortunate class of humanity known as heathen, finds himself regarded, at least by one sect of these very heathen, in a similar light. The discovery is not flattering to his *amour-propre* and shows him that the sentiment in question is not a monopoly of the Christian."

But it was not the illuminating or aesthetic experiences that gave zest to their remarkable Indian journey; rather it was the unforeseen obstacles they were able to overcome. The Indian servant they sent ahead by railway with extra trunks and provisions more often than not failed to find them food and accommodations. They cycled through the Bombay Presidency during an epidemic of plague; went for long stretches without food or water in punishing heat; fought mosquitos; mended as many as forty tire punctures in a day; tucked their boots under their pillows to keep the rats from chewing them up; and spent countless sweltering nights dozing

Fanny on one of her bicycle trips in India.

fitfully on straight-backed wooden chairs in noisy railway-station waiting rooms. And they relished it all, carefully reminding their readers of the differences between themselves and mere tourists or European colonials. The latter, they wrote, lived with three fears: "'a touch of the sun,' fever and 'catching a chill.'" The hardy Workmans dismissed the complaints of these displaced Europeans: "We may say briefly that, in spite of constant exposure to heat, cold, wet, and malaria emanations, in the course of many thousand miles of travel in all parts of India, we escaped all these evils." This was even more remarkable because by now the Workmans were well past their youth. Fanny was thirty-eight and William fifty. A young British lieutenant they met at Ootacumund, in the Nilgiri Hills, remarked "that a woman who could cycle seventy-five miles in a day in the Madras Presidency need fear no heat she might meet in other parts of India." Fanny noted laconically, "This was consoling."

In order to pass one hot season in 1898 before touring India again, they cycled up to Srinagar in Kashmir and made an expedition into the Karakoram and Himalayan mountain ranges. Suddenly their *raison d'être* came into focus. Against the challenge of these towering summits and some of the world's longest glaciers, their journeys on the Indian plains and Deccan paled. That fall they cycled down from Darjeeling, the Bengali hill station. One stretch was a grand downward run of 7,000 feet in 38 miles. They forded four rivers in water above their knees, carrying bicycles and baggage, and finally reached the plains of Bengal. Sitting in the stifling heat under a banyan tree to have their lunch they mused: "Thousands plod up the Brevent each summer to see Mont Blanc and its aiguilles while probably not one person in a year visits this spot on the old Darjeeling turnpike whence one has but to glance northward to behold Everest . . . the world's highest summit, floating up from a mellow haze to an unappreciable height, while a bit to the east rises Janu, a splendid pile of 25,000 feet succeeded by Kanchenjunga, the near rival of K2, effacing the sky with its chalky white wall of over 28,000 feet. These and many others including the Karakoram giants make what the Anglo-Indian calls 'the snows.' Here are snowy towers in comparison with which the much vaunted summits of Switzerland are in truth but Alps."

The incubation period for their grand passion was now over: They put away their trusty Rovers to climb the giants.

That summer of 1898, Fanny and William had first journeyed by foot and later on ponies and yaks through the western Himalaya and Karakoram mountains up to the frontier of Turkestan. In the middle of September they arrived in Darjeeling, at the eastern end of the Himalaya, to make an expedition into Sikkim. They had chosen Darjeeling as a staging center because it was only fifteen hours by rail from the port of Calcutta. They had with them a Swiss guide from Zermatt, their "tents and mountain outfit ordered in London expressly for this expedition, and provisions for two months carefully packed in convenient coolie loads." Their intention was to follow up the Singalila spur of the formidable Kanchenjunga peak, where Nina Mazuchelli had explored in her Barielly dandy thirty years earlier. Then they would cross the Guicha La or pass into the region behind Kanchenjunga, and from there go across Sikkim to the mountains bordering Bhutan on the east. It was an ambitious plan doomed to failure. Obstacles abounded. Sikkim, notorious as the rainiest mountain region in India, was still having stormy afternoons well after the monsoons should have ceased. The government authorities were "disinclined to grant the necessary passes and assistance to persons whose ambitions contemplate investigation of the heights bordering on the forbidden lands of Nepal and Tibet." And the "Political Officer said a good deal about the difficulties of the route, of the density of the rhododendron forests beyond the Guicha La, of the obstruction caused by rivers, of steep and slippery paths, etc., which would make the proposed route almost impassable for a woman." The Workmans assured the officers that they "were accustomed to such difficulties as he mentioned and would take all risks." Eventually it was arranged. Forty-five coolies were secured and equipped at Fanny and William's expense, "each with cap, jersey, woolen trousers, gloves, socks, *putties*, boots, thick woolen blanket and snow glasses." They were to be provisioned for eight weeks and "fifteen more coolies were to be paid and provisioned to carry supplies for the forty-five." But troubles began at once. "Stories of fabulous wealth, of millionaires," floated through the bazaar. Provisions had to be purchased at wildly inflated prices. Not until October 3 were all arrangements completed. By then the daylight hours were decreasing and cold weather was imminent. The coolies were maddeningly indifferent to Fanny and William's 6 a.m. marching orders. They dawdled and hung back, would not bring food and water or pitch tents without endless cajoling, and seldom marched more than five miles a day. At that rate it would have taken the Workmans more than three months to accomplish what they had planned. They tried threats, declaring the coolies "should not have a mouthful of mutton" until their marching shaped up. All to no avail. At the snow line the coolies refused to go on, and there was nothing to do but turn back.

On the second day of their return march, Fanny and William made a long noon halt to wait for the coolies to catch up. When by 3 p.m. only a few had appeared, the Workmans went on, telling those who had showed to hurry the rest along. But it became dark before they were able to reach the government bungalow. "The moonless night fell cloudy and black," they wrote. "We could not see five feet ahead. A cold wind chilled us to the bone." Their lanterns, food and extra clothing were behind with the coolies. The path they were following "descended sharply along a narrow arête. It wound among projecting rocks, was crossed by gigantic tree roots, and was bordered on either side by precipices. Moreover, the steady rain of the afternoon had converted its softer portions into slippery sloughs, so that it was dangerous to travel on even by day." After 10 p.m., four of the coolies appeared and shortly afterwards two others came up from the ramshackle bungalow below with torches and told them their Swiss guide had fallen and cut his head. They stumbled on "over stones and roots, letting ourselves down over washed-out hollows by holding on to bushes and grass." Finally they reached the bungalow and there they sat the night, "without food or bedding." It was the culmination of an embittering experience. "Before a season of marching in the Himalayas is half over," they avowed, "one becomes indifferent to coolie woes." Their attitude was set. In none of their expeditions did they ever establish a rapport with the porters upon whom they were so dependent. Consequently they suffered enormous inconvenience, irritation and expense. Later in the Karakoram, when they had "one of the largest private explorer's caravans ever made up," 150 of their coolies deserted in the night, carrying off a huge supply of grain.

Fanny and William did not have time to develop the skills for dealing with local people that the old Indian hands, abetted by the omniscient authority of the British Raj, had brought to perfection. In India the British quickly grasped the nuances of caste and class because they were themselves the products of an extremely class-conscious society. They understood the master-servant relationship in a way that Americans, coming from a relatively open society, never could. The Workmans, like most of their countrymen, plunged into their enterprises headlong, expecting their enormous energy to overcome all obstacles. They were justifiably criticized by the British for their callous, incompetent behavior toward the Indians. Subtlety and persuasion were not their style.

"We labored under a great disadvantage during our Himalaya travel," they declared, "in not possessing a sufficient mastery of Hindustani to talk freely with the officials of the different tribes we were thrown among." It was entirely different from their European and North African experiences when they understood the language and everyone's actions were clear; when they could fling a cheery "Bien fait!" to a gun-brandishing Algerian bicyclist who overtook them in the Atlas Mountains, knowing he was intent only on racing. In Asia nothing was comprehensible; neither side understood the other. "The advantage of being able to make one's arrangement directly with the chief men, and not through the medium of interpreters, who understand but a few words of English, and are difficult to obtain at that, is obvious." Their patience was tried. Testy, stubbornly obtuse regarding the "intractable Asians," they abandoned Sikkim. But it was a wrench. The views "were something not to be forgotten." Rapturously they wrote, "To the west, far within Nepal, Everest, with its giant sisters, rose straight and creamy from a lapis lazuli plinth of hill and cloud." In one sweeping glance they could see the great peaks of Sikkim and Tibet, mountains they yearned to climb but would never reach. To refresh themselves from this disappointment rather than retreat to Europe that summer of 1898 they made a bicycle tour of Java, but did not write about it.

Undaunted by their failure in Sikkim, they returned the following summer to the Karakoram. This vast mountain range to the west of the Himalaya was in the provinces of Ladakh and Baltisan in an area designated on the old Survey of India maps as Little Tibet.[2] Here, among the highest mountains in the world, peaks seldom dipped below 18,000 feet and often soared above 25,000 feet. Glaciers were long and unexplored.

The Workmans were enticed. Fanny was forty years old and William was fifty-two. They were at the beginning of the great period in their lives. In the next fourteen years, between 1899 and 1912, they led six major expeditions into this remote region they were destined to pioneer. And in the ice-wilds of the Karakoram, Fanny Bullock Workman became in her own right a notable explorer and mountaineer.

Travelers of course had been there before them. Legends told of Alexander the Great's men venturing as far as the Hunza Valley. Buddhist missionaries who spread the faith from India to Eastern Turkestan and China had struggled around the northwest corner of the Himalaya, then across the Tibetan highlands. In the seventeenth and eighteenth centuries Jesuit missionaries made some amazing journeys over difficult passes, but they left scanty and often inaccurate records. It was the British, in the nineteenth century, who began the systematic survey of the Himalaya and Karakoram. Travelers' tales were unreliable, and the British wanted to know the exact topography, the sources of rivers and the accessible passes. Britain was playing "the Great Game" in Asia with Russia—each was extending as far as possible her influence in these autonomous, forbidden regions. In 1821 the British began their Great Trigonometrical Survey of India. Colonel Godwin-Austen, Captain Younghusband and the great explorer Sir Martin Conway preceded the Workmans into the Karakoram, but when Fanny and William set out in 1899 there were still vast blanks on the Survey maps. With characteristic impatience, they sought to fill in as many as they could. Fanny entered into a vigorous correspondence with the Survey and "worked in helpful harmony" with it, according to Sir Sidney Burrard, superintendent of Trigonometrical Surveys. "I should be obliged," she wrote, "if you could tell me whether the Survey regards the Hindu Kush as the westerly extension of the Karakoram range. I should be glad to know this before I refer to it."[3] Differences between the Survey and mountaineers over place names inevitably occurred. Dr. T. G. Longstaff, a distinguished British explorer, objected, before a public meeting in London of the Royal Geographic Society, to the Survey name

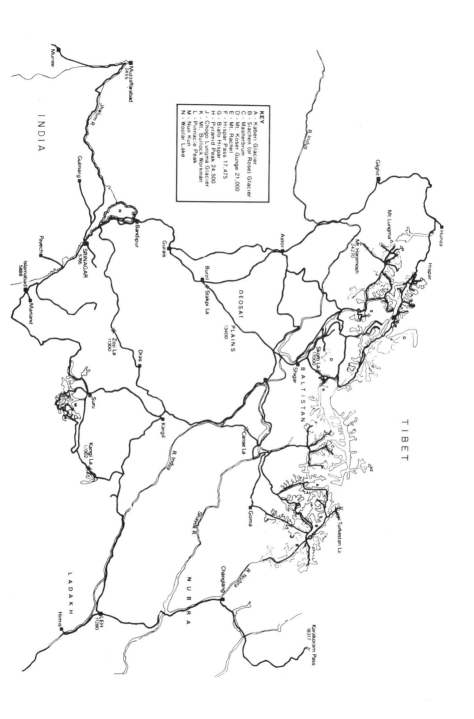

KEY
A - Kaberi Glacier
B - Siachen (or Rose) Glacier
C - Masherbrum
D - Mt. Koser Gunge 21,000
E - Mt. Rachel
F - Hispar Pass 17,475
G - Biato Hispar
H - Pyramid Peak 24,500
J - Chogo Lungma Glacier
K - Mt. Bullock Workman
L - Pinnac.e Peak
M - Nun Kun
N - Woolar Lake

of Bilafond La, a pass in the Karakoram. Weight was given to long usage and the names common among the local people so "It can be realized how the Survey accepted the name from Mrs. Bullock Workman," Sir Sidney explained. Fanny's reputation was growing. She sent letters in every direction, wrote articles for geographic and mountaineering magazines, and named mountains. Objections were raised, "but not by the Survey," Sir Sidney declared, "to the designations . . . given to peaks observed by the Bullock-Workman expeditions."[4]

As early as 1899 Fanny set her first altitude record for women by climbing the 21,000-foot Mt. Koser Gunge. Triumphantly she wrote a separate chapter and signed her name to it in her and William's first mountaineering book, *In the Ice World of the Himalaya* (1900). It was an exhortation:

> For the benefit of women, who may not yet have ascended to altitudes above 16,000 feet but are thinking of attempting to do so, I will here give my experiences for what they are worth. Within four weeks of the completion of a rather exhausting cycle trip in tropical Java, where for six weeks, in a moist temperature varying from 80° to 95° Fahr., I began the march from Srinagar to Baltistan. I had been doing little walking, with the exception of climbing a few Javan volcanoes, which was not invigorating exercise even at heights of 11,000 and 12,000 feet. Two weeks and a half after leaving Batavia were spent in lying around inactive on the decks of steamers, on the train crossing the heated plains of India, in a temperature of 104° to 107° Fahr. for seventy-two hours at Rawal Pindi, and in a *tonga* from that place to Srinagar. It will thus be seen that, in starting out, I was in no especial training for mountain work.
>
> I am not a light weight and am a slow climber. Still my powers of endurance on long days of climbing, and in weeks of continued cycle touring, have, for a number of years, been good. I had been told by people in England and also in

India, that I should not be able to cycle more than one cold weather in the plains, and certainly should not be fit for much in the mountains after a long season of exposure to the sun at lower altitudes. As a matter of fact, my hardest and highest mountain work was accomplished after two seasons, of six months each, cycling in Ceylon, India, and Java.

She did concede, however, that she "experienced much greater difficulty in breathing" at the first high pass of 17,000 feet than later on at 18,000 and 19,000 feet, which suggested to her the "advisability of passing a month, if possible, in valleys of 11,000 to 12,000 feet up. . . . As good a bodily condition as possible is, of course, desirable," she affirmed, "to enable one to combat successfully the factor *majeure* in high climbing, diminished oxygen, as well as to endure fatigue and the extreme cold often met with at high altitudes." Amazingly she "noticed no unpleasant sensations from rarefied air" except "the usual quick breathing, which climbing always causes in my case," nor did she "feel the least desire for kola biscuit, peppermint or cognac, at high altitudes." While Fanny recorded no "mountain sickness," she did have trouble sleeping soundly above 16,000 feet and "at 17,900, our highest camp, my night's rest was often broken in upon by difficulty of breathing." At 19,450 feet her headache subsided, "after a substantial breakfast, for which my appetite was good." During one descent from 21,000 feet, high winds and deep snow reduced her, William's and their European guide's progress to about 300 feet per hour. The strenuous effort made Fanny gasp for oxygen and as she "did not endure severe cold well at any altitude," she found at this great height "the chill and numbness produced by the ice wind bitter to bear." Exhausted as she was when she reached camp that night, she noted that "No lameness resulted." Bouncing back with her usual resilience she wrote, "the following day I felt perfectly fit and able to attack another mountain had it been necessary."

Fanny probably undervalued her own superior physical strength and endurance. Certainly she underestimated the anti-

119

pathetic attitudes of her generation toward sportswomen. Her enthusiasim failed to arouse followers. No other women climbers braved the mountains of Tibet until well after World War I, when modern equipment coupled with team climbing enhanced the success and reduced the risk of such ventures. When Fanny and William made their expeditions, there was very little special mountaineering equipment. They carried flannel-lined Mummery tents with ground sheets sewn in and well padded eider sleeping sacks enclosed in outer ones of camel hair or army blankets, but found them inadequate to keep out the cold even when they slept with all their clothing on. There were no tough, lightweight synthetic tents or ropes, no radios and compact cameras and instruments, and no dehydrated food, oxygen or Prevetine tablets to relieve their bodily needs. They took heavy, cumbersome Kodak equipment and scientific instruments, screwed steel nails into the soles of their boots and wore heavy tweed clothes, pervious to the icy winds and leaden when wet. "Mountaineering in the Himalayas is quite a different thing to mountaineering in Switzerland and the Tyrol," they asserted. "In the Himalayas, there are no villages and hotels within a few hours' distance of summits, no shelter huts, where a climber may break the journey and spend a fairly comfortable night, no corps of guides, who in case of need are ready to render assistance." In the Alps an ascent was usually done in two stages: the first day going to the hut, the second completing the climb and returning to the hut, or even to the valley. "In the Himalayas," the Workmans pointed out, "the mountaineer must go, fully provided with mountain and camp outfit, many days' march beyond even semicivilized villages, into savage and trackless wastes that surround the giants he would conquer. He must brave fatigue, wet, cold, wind and snow, and the effects of altitude, for the bases of many peaks rest upon buttresses that are higher than the summit of Mont Blanc." Just to organize and supervise these expeditions involved an enormous amount of effort and attention to details. Supplies and outfits had to be purchased in Europe, sent by ship to India well ahead of the Workmans' arrival, then on by railway to Srinagar in Kashmir, where they were collected and the damages assessed. Then came the monumental problems of establishing a commissariat service for themselves, hiring assistants, servants, coolies and porters. They always hired one or two European guides for their expert knowledge of snow and ice conditions, but once underway the Workmans bore the entire responsibility for every small decision, for determining their routes in the barren unmapped territory, making scientific observations and taking photographs to illustrate their books. "All this," they wrote, "without authority inherited or delegated." No government or geographical society sponsored them. It was their own driving urge that carried them over every obstacle. Exploration was a way of life they had chosen and could afford. They felt a kinship with others possessed as they were: "When our despair was blackest, we took to reading a traveler's account of how he tried to reach Lhasa and failed." In the vast wilderness and solitude of the mountains, there were tremendous avalanches of snow and rock that thundered down at all hours, immense landslips, "perpendicular walls towering thousands of feet above the valleys . . . vast fields of snow, arêtes and domes of snow crowning inaccessible rock massifs." They struggled with the effects of altitude: impaired judgment and overwhelming lassitude, fearing that "the next howling wind should rend the tents from their moorings." With all this, by their own statement, they were happy and knew why: "Forgetting the trials that the treading of unexplored paths must needs bring, we sympathize fully with McCormick's quotation, 'Think of the people who are presenting their compliments, and requesting the honor, and 'much regretting'; of those that are pinioned at dinner tables, or stuck up in ballrooms, or cruelly planted in pews; aye think of these, and so remembering how many poor devils are living in a state of utter respectability, you will glory the more in your own delightful escape.'"

Fanny and William's eight mountaineering escapes were recorded in five thick books: *In the Ice World of the Himalaya* (1900), *Ice Bound Heights of the Mustagh* (1908), *Peaks and Glaciers of the Nun Kun* (1909), *The Call of the Snowy Hispar* (1910), *Two Summers in the Ice Wilds of the Eastern Karakoram* (1917). They

121

wrote all but one of the books in collaboration, as they had done with the bicycling books. All of their expeditions were based on a division of duties. One year Fanny would take charge of the planning and organizing of the expedition and William would prepare for the scientific and photographic projects. The next year they would reverse their roles. It was a harmonious arrangement, free of competition, based on mutual support as they attested in numerous references.

In 1902 and 1903, the Workmans made two major expeditions to explore and map the thirty-mile-long Chogo Lungma glacier and its affluents in northern Baltistan. At the head of the glacier Fanny climbed Mt. Lungma (22,568 feet) and broke her own altitude record. William scaled Pyramid Peak, setting a world record for men at 23,392 feet. He was fifty-six years old.

The peak and glacier group of the Nun Kun, southwest of Srinagar in Kashmir, was the object of their 1906 expedition. "The enthusiasm" of Fanny "for what she undertook was unbounded," William wrote with unabashed admiration. "She concentrated her attention on the end in view, often disregarding the difficulties and even the dangers that might lie in the way of accomplishment. She went forward with a determination to succeed and a courage that won success where a less determined effort would have failed. She believed in taking advantage of every opportunity. She was no quitter, and was never the first to suggest turning back in the face of discouraging circumstances. She frequently urged her Alpine guides on to renewed effort where they began to hesitate." On the Nun Kun expedition Fanny made her great ascent of Pinnacle Peak in the Nun Kun massif which she measured as 23,300 feet. By this achievement, she remarked joyfully, she "won a place with Dr. Workman in the small band of mountaineers who have reached a height of over 23,000 feet." She was forty-seven years old. Later triangulations by the Survey placed the height at 22,810 feet, but it was high enough to remain for twenty-eight years a world's altitude record for women.

Setting records exhilarated the Workmans. Their Camp America in the Nun Kun at 21,000 feet was at the time the highest point that mountaineers had passed a night. There, they found, "The air was silent with mountain stillness more potent than speech. . . . For what has Nature more truly significant than the great icy mountains and the star-sprinkled sky?" It was their chosen, beloved domain.

"Of great importance for the knowledge of this world of icy mountains are the several journeys undertaken by Dr. Hunter Workman and Mrs. Bullock Workman," wrote the famous Swedish explorer Sven Hedin in his exhaustive twelve-volume study, *Southern Tibet.*[5] Lured by unmapped glaciers as well as unconquered peaks, Fanny and William devoted their 1908 expedition to an exploration of the complicated, thirty-eight-mile-long Hispar Glacier in the Hunza Nagar region, partly because "we had a hobby for finding a new pass, over which a caravan could be taken to the Hispar." They succeeded in crossing the Hispar Pass (17,500 feet) and descending the thirty-seven-mile-long Biafo Glacier. Traversing the two glaciers joined at the Hispar Pass constituted a total ice journey of seventy-five miles—another record. Prior to this achievement, Fanny had written in the *National Geographic Magazine* that she was "the only woman who has made the first ascent of one of the great Himalayan glaciers or any other of equal size." She was the preeminent female trail-blazer, zealously building her reputation. That any other woman should challenge her altitude record aroused her to monumental indignation. Another American, Miss Annie Peck, claimed to have reached 23,000 and probably 24,000 feet on Mount Huascarán in Peru in 1908. Outraged, Fanny enlisted the aid of M. Henri Valliot of the Société Générale d'Études et de Travaux Topographiques of Paris and in 1909 sent at her own expense an expedition to Peru under the direction of M. Etienne de Larminant of the Service Geographique de l'Armes, to measure the mountain in question. The French engineers made "a thorough and accurate triangulation of the two summits of Mount Huascarán." As Fanny pointed out in a letter to the editor of the *Scientific American,* poor Miss Peck had made only eye estimates of the mountain's height. Fanny's expedition demolished Miss Peck's claim. In a handsomely bound report with numerous maps and diagrams, the observations and calculations proved the two Andes summits to be 21,812 feet and 22,182 feet. So, she concluded jubilantly, "they show that the altitude of the lower summit of Huascarán, claimed to have been ascended by Miss Peck, is some 1500 feet lower than the highest altitude atained by Mrs. Bullock Workman." Miss Peck replied in the pages of *Scientific American*[6] that she had not expected the scientific world to take her estimate as an exact measurement, though "It was, of course, quite within the province of anyone to take so great an interest in the matter as to spend some thousands of dollars in sending engineers to Peru to make a triangulation of the mountain, and to publish this as the absolute height of Huascarán." Allowances for refraction in triangulation had to be made, she argued, and in Peru, where the atmosphere was much drier than in India, a mountain so measured might prove to be 1,000 to 2,000 feet higher than figured. Fanny did not reply.

The Workmans continued to make their scientific studies with complete confidence. They made observations of the physiological effects of high altitude. They studied the structure, movement and particular phenomena of ice and glaciers, and the nature and development of ice pinnacles. They took maximum and minimum sun and shade temperatures, prismatic compass observations, and altitude measurements with both aneroid barometers and boiling point thermometers. In 1911, they explored and mapped glaciers in Baltisan, around Mount Masherbrum, an area to which later mountaineers were drawn. They crossed the ice-covered Bilaphond Pass (18,000 feet) and made a descent to the great Siachen or Rose Glacier. It should have been enough. Fanny was now fifty-two years old and William sixty-four. But their passions were still aroused by the challenge of the unknown. Fanny explained: '"No, I won't come again,' I said, as I sat snowed in my tent for two days before returning over the Bilaphond La in September 1911. But no sooner had I turned my back to the Rose Glacier and reached again the top of the pass on that brilliant September 16th, than my mountain-ego reasserted itself, saying *tant pis* to the obstacles, 'Return you must.'"

And return they did. The 1912 expedition, their last, was made on Fanny's initiative. The seductive, nearly inaccessible Siachen Glacier had lured her back and Fanny explored its entire length— forty-five miles—to its source on the watershed between the Indus and Turkestan basins. "Dr. Hunter Workman accompanied me," she wrote, "this time, in charge with me of commissariat and as photographer and glacialist, but I was the responsible leader of this expedition, and on my efforts, in a large measure, must depend the success or failure of it." She secured the services of Mr. C. Grant Peterkin of the Royal Geographical Society as surveyor and Mr. Sarjan Singh from the Indian Survey to assist him. The Royal Society and the Survey loaned her plane-tables, chronometer watches and other valuable instruments. Cyprien Savoye of Pré St. Didier, Italy, who had been with the Workmans on four previous expeditions was hired and with him Quaizier Siméon and Rey Adolph, also Italian guides, and Chenoz Césare and Rey Julian, Italian porters. All had Himalayan as well as Alpine experience.

One sparkling, sunlit morning everyone's spirits were high and the Workmans and their guides were looking forward to the climb ahead. Chenoz had thought the snow was in excellent condition. The surface seemed solid and free from crevasses. In a carefree mood he laughed at the advisability of roping together. What the porter did not see as they strode along was a streak of slightly depressed, yellow-tinged snow—a crucial warning. One step ahead of Fanny, Chenoz suddenly disappeared. She stood paralyzed, gazing into the icy blue fathomless hole at her feet.

That night was a ghastly one; the expedition was overcome with grief. They sat up until near dawn agonizing over what to do. Ultimately, Fanny recalled, "all appreciated that the work of the expedition must be carried on at once. . . . My own escape from sharing his [Chenoz's] dire fate was quite miraculous. Those who share the Oriental belief in 'Kismet' might say his passing was fore-ordained, while others, believing in the 'survival of the fittest,' have said that I, having the work to carry on, was, by not taking one step more, and by chance not being roped, saved to accomplish it. *Qui sait?*"

Garbled reports of the tragedy filtered through the villages back to the European and American press so that later the Workmans had the macabre experience of reading some 300 of their own obituary notices. Fanny led the expedition on and crossed a pass, Sia La, (18,700 feet) near the head of the Siachen Glacier and made a descent through a wholly unknown snow region to the Kaberi Glacier. Sven Hedin wrote that the "fascinating book" that detailed the expedition "is one of the most important contributions ever given to our knowledge of these mountains."[7] It was Fanny's triumph. Even Kenneth Mason, a constant critic of the Workmans and one-time superintendent of the Survey of India and Professor of Geography, Oxford, conceded that the "results of this expedition are in an entirely different category" from their earlier ventures: all the "prominent peaks along the Shaksgam watershed were fixed for position and height," and this was "a fine achievement."[8] The famous Sir Martin Conway conceded in convoluted prose that there was criticism of Fanny and William in certain English quarters, but was obliged to conclude that they had added "enormously to our knowledge of the greatest knot or group of mountains on the face of Earth."[9]

Two Summers in the Ice Wilds of Eastern Karakoram that covered the 1911 and 1912 expeditions was the only book Fanny and William did not write jointly. Fanny told the 1912 story herself in Part II: "The Conquest of the Great Rose, or Siachen, The World's Longest Non-Polar Glacier." Among the 141 excellent photographs in the book is a marvelous one of Fanny captioned, "On Silver Throne plateau at nearly 21,000 feet." Standing in a skirt, jacket and sun helmet, her ice-axe stuck in the snow in front of her, was Fanny reading a newspaper with the headline: VOTES FOR WOMEN.

It was an unremitting struggle throughout her mountaineering and exploring career for Fanny to be taken seriously. She knew the stings of the battle to be accepted and recognized in a man's world. Eventually she received numerous honors and some fame, but acceptance was more elusive. Summarizing her life, the editor of the English *Alpine Journal* wrote that she was "a very doughty fighter, as, indeed, became her pure New England ancestry." He conceded that "She herself felt she suffered from 'sex antagonism' and it is possible that some unconscious feeling, let us say of the novelty of a woman's intrusion into the domain of exploration so long reserved to man, may in some quarters have existed."[10]

Through it all William was her loyal supporter, his faith never faltering in her ability to cope as an absolute equal with him. "The Doctor wielded a pretty blade," the same editor wrote, "never so keen or quick as in her support." But he paid a price: "Thus in time there tended to arise in certain high and serene circles an atmosphere, shall we say, of aloofness?" Fanny's "warmness of heart, her enthusiasm, her humor, her buoyant delight in doing," were all acknowledged by the *Alpine* editor. But these were not enough to overcome the enormity of her transgression.

Assiduously Fanny collected her credentials throughout her career as if sheer number of affiliations would guarantee her acceptance in the circles that counted. She was a Fellow of the Royal Geographic Society, of the Royal Scottish Geographical Society and a member of the Royal Asiatic Society; Grand Medalist of the Alpin Français; Membre d'Honneur des Sociétés de Géographie de Belge, Nancy, Marseilles, d'Alger et de l'Afrique Nord; a charter member of the American Alpine Club; Honorary Member, Appalachian Mountain Club; Corresponding Member, Brooklyn Institution of Arts and Science, The National Geographic Society, and the K. K. Geographische Gesellschaft of Vienna. She was a member of the Club Alpino Italiano, The Ladies Alpine Club (London), the Lyceum Club; the Cyclists' Touring Club of Great Britain and the Touring Club de France. She was designated an Officier de l'Instruction Publique et Beaux Arts de France at the request of President Loubet in 1904, and she was the first American woman to lecture at the Sorbonne.

Perhaps her greatest victory was breaching that masculine province of ultimate recognition, the Royal Geographical Society. When she lectured before the Society in 1905, she was the second woman to do so since its founding in 1830. Isabella Bird Bishop had been the first. When William spoke there—and it was rumored she wrote his speeches—Fanny was away on a whirlwind tour of her own, from Vienna to Hamburg, delivering thirty lectures in thirty-seven days. William wrote that she "was greatly interested in the higher education of women and in their advancement to an equality with men in social, literary, scientific, and political fields." In her will she left a total of $125,000 to four women's colleges: Bryn Mawr, Radcliffe, Smith and Wellesley. Her Bryn Mawr bequest, augmented by a gift from William, established the Fanny Bullock Workman Traveling Fellowship.

The First World War delayed the publication of the Workmans' final book until 1917. To it Fanny appended a note:

> While it is not claimed for the map of the Siachen or Rose Glacier that it is final and cannot be improved upon in some particulars in the future, it is today the only one representing with considerable accuracy the topographical features of the very important area which it covers.
>
> The object of placing my full name in connection with the expedition on the map, is not because I wish in any way to thrust myself forward, but solely that in the accomplishments of women, now and in the future, it should be known to them and stated in print that a woman was the initiator and special leader of this expedition. When, later, woman occupies her acknowledged position as an individual worker in all fields, as well as those of exploration, no such emphasis of her work will be needed; but that day has not fully arrived, and at present it behooves women, for the benefit of their sex, to put what they do, at least, on record.
>
> In stating this I do not wish to ignore or underrate the valuable cooperation on this expedition of my husband and joint worker, Dr. W. Hunter Workman.

Fanny and William went to the south of France during World War I. There, after a long and painful illness, Fanny died in Cannes, on January 22, 1925, at the age of sixty-six. "Altogether few women of the times," wrote Arthur Tarbell in the *New England*

Magazine, "have done so much as Mrs. Workman, and done it so well."[11]

William returned to Newton, Massachusetts. He lived to the age of ninety-one, a respected explorer devoted to the memory and reputation of his valiant and indefatigable Fanny. He called her his greatest friend as well as his beloved wife. As a pioneer she was presumptuous. But as a wife she was a rare example of a successful, equal partner in a life-long collaboration. A colleague who saw beyond the controversy Fanny caused wrote of her and William "that among us who know the great mountains her name and his will ever be linked together as having done great things and deserved well of their generation."[12]

*"Marche comme ton coeur te mene et
selon le regard de tes yeux."*
l'Ecclesiaste
(Favorite verse of Alexandra David-Neel)

III. FRENCH SCHOLAR ADVENTURER:

ALEXANDRA DAVID-NEEL (1868-1969)

I

ALEXANDRA DAVID-NEEL BECAME A legend in her own time. She was an Orientalist, a prodigious traveler in the East and a fountainhead of esoteric knowledge. In the disguise of a Tibetan beggar woman she lived and traveled among the peoples of China and Tibet as no Western woman had ever done before. As a Buddhist scholar and teacher she was welcomed in homes and monasteries. She read and spoke Tibetan flawlessly and was the first European woman to enter the forbidden city of Lhasa.

Much honored in her old age, Alexandra played the role of the *grande dame* with relish—being alternately charming and terrible-tempered, ebullient and despotic. Photographs of her as a little white-haired, bright-eyed woman impart her air of success and confidence.

As a girl, however, Alexandra appeared shy and vulnerable—almost a beauty but for the hurt, lost look that clouded her delicate features. In her early photographs there is no hint of the dogged determination that transformed her from a genteel bourgeoise girl into the daring adventurer in the wild lands of Central Asia. Even

Alexandra David as a young woman.

later her expression retained something of the wariness of her youth. When she was fifty-six years old and had just completed one of the most remarkable journeys in the annals of exploration, she had her photograph taken in Calcutta to commemorate the event. Her preparation for this moment had been long and often painful. But the picture does not show her in one of those triumphant hands-on-hips, shoulders-back poses so typical of the early male explorers. She simply stands there in Tibetan dress with her pack on her back, walking stick in one hand and begging bowl in the other, looking remarkably young and a bit tentative. Her face no longer has the sadness of her youth. She is still watchful, only more intent.

This picture was on the dust jacket of Alexandra's book *My Journey to Lhasa*, first published (in America) in 1927. Later she translated it into French for publication in Paris. It was her second book, but the first to be enthusiastically received and widely reviewed. For the next forty years the books and articles that poured from David-Neel's prolific pen had a faithful audience and brought her a small but steady income. Completely self-disciplined, she wrote every day, and age would not diminish her energy. Eighteen days before she died, in her 101st year, she painfully scribbled, "Je ne peux plus écrire"—I am not able to write anymore. The incredible journey was over. Her life had begun obscurely, and was nearly lost in the destructive morass of despair. Then, belatedly, she burst forth in a full flowering beyond any early expectations. At the crisis point of her life Alexandra had confronted the problem of fulfilling her potential. With unusual self-knowledge she chose the right path for the realization of her rare talents: a path without guideposts, fraught with obstacles and adventures few women have ever encountered.

Alexandra David was the only child of Alexandrine Borghmans, a Belgian, and Louis Pierre David, a Frenchman.[1] Louis David, a native of Tours, became a school teacher but his intense interest in politics ultimately claimed him; some time in the 1840's he left teaching for journalism and founded a revolutionary journal. At this time Victor Hugo was the powerful leader of the second Romantic generation in France. When Hugo fled to Brussels after

Louis Napoleon's coup d'état of December 1851, David, who was forced into exile for his political activities, followed him. Alexandra recalled that as a child Victor Hugo had bounced her on his knee. But there were so many passionate French political activists concentrated in Brussels that the Belgian government felt it prudent to disperse them. Louis David was allowed to live in the charming university town of Louvain. Here, at the age of forty, he married twenty-year-old Alexandrine, the daughter of a teacher but completely devoid of David's intellectual and political fervor. When, after sixteen years of unhappy marriage, they were to have a baby, David obtained permission to return to Paris so that the child might be born a French citizen on French soil. Louise Eugenié Alexandrine Marie was born at Sainte-Mandé, a suburb of Paris, October 24, 1868. Three days later she was baptized in the parish church, Notre-Dame de Saint-Mondé.[2]

No rosy remembrances of a happy childhood remained with Alexandra David-Neel. Throughout life she was consistent in her view that she had suffered a great deal from neglect and want of love. The tensions between her mismatched parents can only be imagined. If Louis David craved "*la grande passion*" that Victor Hugo so eloquently advocated and exemplified, he apparently did not find it with his wife. Quite likely he shared with other French romantics an elitism that fostered the desire to make an impression. The cult of the individual, the expression of the ego, the insistence on the primacy of feeling, the exploration of the unconscious, were all much in vogue. Alexandra admired her father and through him was rooted in the romantic tradition. But he was old when she was born, a bit aloof and unreceptive to the needs of his sensitive daughter.

Alexandra felt totally rejected by her mother, who she claimed was interested only in social trivia. Her greatest fear was that she would resemble her. Looking in the mirror at the age of thirty-seven, she wrote that she did not recognize her own body, that she saw wrinkles in her face, grey in her hair, and to her horror every day she appeared more like her mother: in her face were "those features which I hate."

Alexandra recalled a lonely, restrictive childhood:

Ever since I was five years old, a tiny precocious child of Paris, I wished to move out of the narrow limits in which, like all children of my age, I was then kept. I craved to go beyond the garden gate, to follow the road that passed it by, and to set out for the unknown. But, strangely enough, this "unknown" fancied by my baby mind always turned out to be a solitary spot where I could sit alone, with no one near, and as the road toward it was closed to me I sought solitude behind any bush, any mound of sand, that I could find in the garden, or wherever else my nurse took me.

Later her escape was in books—hours were spent reading Fenimore Cooper and Jules Verne fantasies and books on travel, and poring over maps. Phileas Fogg and his valet Passepartout out of *Around the World in Eighty Days*, the children of Captain Grant, Captain Hatteras and all the other heroes of Jules Verne were her heroes too. She resolved to be like them—if possible, better. She would travel!

As a child Alexandra asserted herself by running away. Looking back, she liked to see her bids for escape as proof that she was a born explorer. One of her favorite stories about herself was how, at the age of five, she eluded her nurse in the Bois de Vincennes. Her parents and the police were alerted, and everyone went in search of the little girl. Night came. At last she was found by a policeman and taken to the police station. There she was asked what she was doing all alone in the Bois and what her name was, but she refused to answer all questions for fear she would be sent home. Thus, as Alexandra was pleased to recount, her first exploration ended in a police station.

"I never asked my parents for any gifts except books on travel, maps, and the privilege of being taken abroad during my school holidays," she declared. "When a girl, I could remain for hours near a railway line, fascinated by the glittering rails and fancying the many lands toward which they led. But, again, my imagination did not evoke towns, buildings, gay crowds or stately pageants; I dreamed of wild hills, immense deserted steppes and impassable landscapes of glaciers!''

Somehow Alexandra's spirit flourished in the uncongenial atmosphere of her early life. From that first escapade in the Bois de Vincennes she made repeated breaks for freedom. She ran away from her convent school several times. At sixteen, when her family vacationed at Ostend, she bolted across the Channel to England where she stayed until her money ran out. At eighteen she walked as far as the Goddard Pass with a volume of Epictetus, the Stoic philosopher, in her pocket. She claimed to be his follower, sleeping on the floor and otherwise inuring herself to hardship and the simple life. Her parents recovered her at the Italian lakes.

As a child Alexandra had been a Catholic and considered becoming a Carmelite nun until she discovered that the convents looked like prisons. After she disavowed Catholicism she became interested in the study of comparative religion, a popular interest fostered by the romantic movement. Buddhism was not very well known in France in Alexandra's time. But there was a Theosophical Society in Paris, established in the eighties, where lectures and discussions on Buddhist and Brahmanic theories were held. Almost all French Orientalists were members. It may have been here that Alexandra first learned about Buddhism. Later she often stayed at the quarters of the Theosophical Society in London, Paris and, eventually, in India.

But it was in the quiet sanctuary of the Musée Guimet, Alexandra said, that she found her vocation. The Musée Guimet is a museum in Paris devoted entirely to antiquities of the Far East. Alexandra remembered it to be a temple with wide stone steps rising between walls covered with sublime frescoes depicting the mysteries of the East—a brahmin tossing an offering into the sacred fire, saffron-robed Buddhist monks with bowls in their outstretched hands, a Japanese temple painted vermillion and a path bordered by pink cherry trees in full bloom. At the top of the stairs was the great library, which Alexandra called her "holy of holies": a dark den dominated by a massive enthroned Buddha, abandoned to his meditations, enigmatic, a faint beatific smile on his smooth features, his body in controlled repose. According to Monsieur Gabriel Monod-Herzen, Professor of Oriental Studies (retired) at the Collège de France and an old friend of Alexandra, she experienced a spiritual revelation before a great statue of Buddha. Perhaps it was this exceptional one in the Musée Guimet.

In the small reading room to the right of the great library the young Alexandra found the solitary retreat she was always seeking. No sounds from the noisy Paris streets penetrated the thick walls; only the gentle flutter of turning pages stirred the quiet air as she pored over books on China, Japan and India and dreamed "of all those places in the world beyond the Suez. . . . Vocations are born," she later wrote. "Mine was born there."

A small inheritance from her godmother enabled Alexandra to make a trip by sea to India and Ceylon (now Sri Lanka) when she was in her early twenties. Her stateroom opened directly onto the deck and she spent the voyage out reading the *Upanishads,* the *Bhagavad-Gita* and Buddhist writings, and contemplating the sea from her cabin door. Fellow passengers were puzzled by this unaccompanied young woman who kept to herself. When they questioned her, she reported, all it took to silence them was answering with a very grave air that she was going to India to continue her study of Sanskrit: she suspected, probably correctly, that her questioners did not know if Sanskrit were a language or a place. She disembarked at Colombo, Ceylon, took rickshaw rides to see the standard sights and eventually crossed the Gulf of Mannar to India, traveling the length and breadth of the subcontinent by train. Writing about this trip nearly half a century later in *L'Inde Où J'ai Vecu,* she declared that she had gone to India to find the contemplative life and to see wise hermits living out in the fresh air perfumed by fragrant forests. Instead she found an India withered and dry, burned by the brutal sun and gripped in the tragedy of famine.

The reality of Asia must have seemed stark and brutal for a girl who had dreamed among the books in the libraries of Paris.

But it did not repel her. That first voyage to India only increased Alexandra's longing for the East.

But she had no income. Her father could not support her because he had lost his money through bad investments in the stock market. So Alexandra had to return to France to earn her own living. It was the 1890's—the unique period in French life known as La Belle Epoque. From the late 1800's until the outbreak of the First World War there was an exhilarating interlude in the artistic life of Paris. Parisians, usually indifferent to serious music, suddenly displayed a startling enthusiasm for all manner of musical events, from the well-known works of Gounod and Massenet to more classical symphonies and operas. Any social function with an artist attending was sure of success. Women were denied any legal rights; they could not enter the professions and there were few respectable ways for them to earn money. But by becoming actresses or singers they could achieve an unprecedented prestige and status. Just as Colette had left the provinces and become an actress in Paris, in the same period Alexandra David became an opera singer. She had shown early promise playing the piano, singing, and composing music, and had been a finalist for the Prix de Rome for composition. Now, in the Paris of the nineties, Jules Massenet wrote Alexandra a letter praising her interpretation of the role of Manon in his operatic masterpiece, *Manon*.

Alexandra traveled with the Opéra-Comique touring company and in 1896 was billed as their "*première chanteuse*" in Hanoi and Haiphong under the pseudonym Mademoiselle Myrial. In 1899 she went to Greece with L'Opéra d'Athènes, then to Tunis in 1902 as a director for the Casino de Tunis. The next year she abandoned theater life for good and took up the same career as her father—journalism. She wrote for both English and French magazines, usually about Buddhism and the East. At this point she wrote to her parents that she wanted to stay in Tunis. She had met her future husband, a distant cousin named Philippe-François Neel.

Philippe was stationed in Tunis as the chief engineer for La Compagnie du Chemin de Fer Bône-Guelma. He was born in Alès in the south of France in 1861, making him seven years

Alexandra's senior. Philippe was an extremely handsome man but by Alexandra's report "very English" and full of himself with a proud demeanor, very "fin de siècle." They knew each other intimately for several years, according to M. Monod-Herzen, and he declared that "There was between them a mutual respect and deep affection which lasted throughout their lives." Yet surely this was the strangest of marriages. On August 3, 1904, Alexandra wrote in her diary, "I married that dreadful *allouche* [Arab for "sheep," an endearing term; Philippe's hair curled like a sheep's] at the Consulate in Tunis." Five days later they sailed for Europe and went their separate ways, she to Paris and he to the south of France. Rather than expressing joy over so significant a step in her life, Alexandra confided to her diary that she felt everything was finished with marriage, that all was over and she was no longer free. For a woman who had made her own living and maintained her independence until she was thirty-six years old, marriage suddenly seemed an unbearable restriction.

Two months later, still in Paris, Alexandra wrote to Mouchy, as she called her husband: "We have made a singular marriage, more out of malice than tenderness. It was foolish, without doubt, but it is done." She would have been sweet to him, she explained in another letter, if he had not cut her down, made fun of her unreasonably and subjected her to such despicable ideas that she lost her way. "I am very unhappy, Mr. Neel," she wrote. "You who promised me such sunlight, why have you cast me into the night?" Ambiguous references are made to another woman—"if she leaves I will return." Yet Alexandra declared she was entirely sympathetic toward both the woman and Philippe, and advised him to be very gentle because women who become dependent upon men place themselves in such a precarious position. Then no more mention is made of the mysterious woman.

At the same time Alexandra's letters to her husband were full of "my dear Mouchy," and "my poor Mouchy" and admonishments for him not to be sad: with intelligence and luck, she said, they would build a good life.

Then a crisis came. On December 20, 1904 within a year of her

Archives A. D-Neel

Philippe Neel

marriage, her father died. Alexandra returned to her parents' home in Brussels and confronted herself.

There was the setting—the familiar furniture, everything to remind her of her unhappy childhood. She was in a state of extreme anxiety. Her father, whom she loved and apparently wished in some way to emulate, was dead. Her mother received her coldly. She was isolated, face to face with her diminished self. In an anguished but amazingly insightful letter to Philippe written in August 1905, Alexandra analyzed why she had come into existence and how, as a misconceived instrument of reconciliation between her parents, she was a mistake. She blamed her mother, who

. . . felt things rather than consciously analyzing them. I am the daughter of the man she did not love. I am his daughter alone in spite of the blood from which she made me and the milk with which she nourished me. . . . See, my friend, that which sometimes awaits those imprudent women who look to maternity for consolation from an ill-matched union. At a certain age shadows of character soften. . . .

In this long and powerful letter Alexandra lamented her "own poverty," her "lapses of spirit . . . that only death, perhaps, will terminate." She saw herself as a wife being pulled inexorably into the self-annihilating role of her mother. If she had a child she would be as destructive toward it as her mother was to her. Despondent as she was, however, she did not lose her hold on life or become mired in despair. Instead, she struggled to claim the potential she felt—that of her father's daughter in her—and she fought to overcome her terror at the possibility of repeating her mother's misery. She knew she needed freedom. With a rare understanding of her own predicament and the potential for disaster in the parental role, she told Philippe why she did not want to have children. From her protest it can be inferred he desired a family. But his natural wish was not her idea of fulfillment:

My son and my daughter, in reliving what I was in earlier times, would be incomprehensible to you and you would not respect them. That would be the sad struggle amidst these children. Indifference would perhaps come on your part, but I am only too fully aware of the mother I would be to risk the terrible adventure. The child for me would be the god to whom would go all my adoration. He would be my unique hope and I would only live to see him live the life I did not live, to realize the ideal I did not attain. Without doubt he would not achieve this. But it could happen that I would become a person in whom lodged a spirit dissimilar to my present one . . . it would be the story of my mother, but intensified by all the superiority, sensitivity and intelligence that I have over that wretched woman in whom disappointments only changed into rancor and spitefulness against her unsuspecting child.

Not only the maternal role but marriage, the conventional life, security itself, Alexandra perceived as stifling to her needs. She described to Philippe what they would become as a married couple:

> Each day we will accept each other more. Each day our mutual indulgence will grow. The ties that will unite us will become stronger. We will get used to the idea of our reciprocal misery and we will console each other as much as we can. That is wisdom.

But it was not the wisdom she wanted. She tried to explain:

> We can place between us a relative peace but how to soften the contact with new souls? How to renounce incarnating in the child one has placed in the world the proud ideal that one has proposed to oneself and by which one has almost always failed? How to support the terrible thought of not being able to expose before him one's life, all of one's life, sentiments and actions, and to have him—in his juvenile enthusiasm, in his vigorous and implacable logic, not yet blunted by life—be a severe judge? Ah, my poor dear, believe me there is much wisdom, much foresight in my will not to be a mother. The difficulties that we create, our divergences of mentality, will attenuate more and more.

In this singularly revealing letter Alexandra was propounding a sophisticated rationale that relieved her of much guilt: she was freeing Philippe, not leaving him. And freedom for her was the most important thing in life. She rejected a passive acceptance of the destiny thrust upon her by circumstances of sex and the historical accident of birth, responding instead to some deep instinct for autonomy. She rebelled against what she considered the tyranny of marriage and parenthood. She had suffered already; she would not be a martyr in marriage and suffer more.

After this unsparing self-analysis Alexandra began in earnest to create her own world. At first it was full of despair. She could not see what direction to take and had thoughts of suicide. Why did he pursue her? she asked Philippe. He was such a prisoner of turn-of-the-century attitudes toward women that she must have seemed like all other women to him—of little worth, only to be dallied with. How could he accuse her of "incommensurable pride" when he was so arrogant himself? Then she pleaded, "Mouchy, give me your hand." The letter he wrote in response must have touched her; she assured him, "You are the best husband one could dream of, I acknowledge it without hesitation and it is for that reason I am tormented by a situation that is also extremely painful for you."

Philippe, with admirable understanding and sensitivity, wrote to her in England that perhaps she would like a voyage to restore her spirits. She answered that it would give her the greatest pleasure; that when she was well enough and properly prepared she would accept his proposal.

After this traumatic period triggered by her father's death, Alexandra and Philippe never established a conventional married life. Alexandra spent most of her time in Paris and London, Philippe in North Africa. She wrote that she would return with pleasure to their seaside retreat in La Goulette near Tunis, but that she could never accept the social responsibilities he expected of a wife. She continued to assure him that he was an excellent husband and she would not exchange him with another: "We are matched socially," she reminded him, "We have relatives in common and we help one another."

For unfathomable reasons Philippe consented to the terms Alexandra demanded in their marriage. He never sought a divorce and continued to support her financially and in every other way until his death nearly forty years later. He transacted all her complicated business matters and arranged to send her money regularly. He accepted the hand-written articles she sent him, had them typed and sent on to the journals she designated. When she traveled he arranged for the shipment of her goods and received what she sent back. When she bought a house in the south of France he looked after its rental, purchased furniture and fittings for it and had his niece inspect it periodically to be sure her things were all right. Often he admonished her not to acquire too much as she always had difficulty with shipments. He congratulated her when her books sold well and kept her informed about his nieces and the state of affairs wherever he was, either in Europe or North Africa. He was her life line, the single link to the world she left behind as she shed her European ways and traveled deeper into Asia. Alexandra, probably having decided that she was destined for fame, asked Philippe to keep her letters and he did: 3,000 typewritten pages now in Mlle. Peyronnet's possession. (She kept few of his.) She had survived what today would be called her identity crisis. Her will was formidable. She shed her bonds and turned to a new life.

II

From 1903 until 1911 Alexandra wrote, studied and traveled in Europe, making only a few short trips to Tunisia to be with Philippe. Her articles appeared in many magazines, particularly the *Mercure de France*, and in 1907 she published her first book: *Socialisme Chinois: Le Philosophe Meh Ti et L'Idée de Solidarité*. It was signed Alexandra David. She also wrote under her psuedonym, Myrial. It was important, she told Philippe, for her to remain distinct from him; not everyone shared her religious beliefs or her political opinions. (She had written earlier an anarchist tract.[3]) It was better for him if she kept a separate identity. Still, she said, if he wished she would give up her pen name. There is no record of Philippe's reply, but all of Alexandra's subsequent books and later articles were signed with their hyphenated surnames, David-Neel.

The trip Philippe had promised her was very much on her mind. She would go once more to India. In preparation she studied Sanskrit, attended classes at the Sorbonne and went to lectures given by Sylvain Levi, an eminent Professor of Oriental Studies at the Collège de France, where in the early 1890's she first heard that other famous Orientalist, Philippe-Edouard Foucaux. She gave lectures herself—on comparative religions— at the Theosophical Societies in London and Paris. And, according to M. Monod-Herzen, she taught at the Université Nouvelle, a private institution in Brussels. But a pedagogical career did not interest her. She explained: "There are great men at the Sorbonne who know all the roots of the words and the historical dates, but I wish to live philosophy on the spot and undergo physical and spiritual training, not just read about them."

Finally Alexandra felt prepared to return to Asia. She left Paris for India on August 3, 1911, unaware that her journey would take nearly fourteen years.

A recurrent theme in Alexandra's letters was her longing for the East. The yearning began in her childhood. When she first went to Indo-China with the Opéra-Comique she immediately felt at home, as if this were the place she should be. Now in India again she began to penetrate deeper into Asian life. She still went to European garden parties, had lunch with the wife of the Governor of Madras, and met Lady Harding, the British Viceroy's wife, in Calcutta. But she also visited ashrams and stayed with Hindu friends in the "native quarter" of Calcutta. Everywhere Alexandra met with Indian philosophers and teachers and often lectured to them. At the College of Sanskrit in the University of Calcutta the professors compared her to Sarasvati, the Hindu goddess of learning, and gave her a special benediction. You cannot imagine the glamor and prestige a European Buddhist enjoys in Asia, she wrote Philippe. "If you were here, dearest, I would embrace you with all my heart for the great joy that you have given me in the autumn of my life by making it possible for me to study the great passion of my youth. . . ." She was forty-two years old and felt, after only a few months in India, that she had collected material for years and years of work.

Early in 1912 Alexandra decided that an interview with the Dalai Lama would make an interesting article in the *Mercure de France*. The Dalai Lama, spiritual head of all Tibetans, had fled from Lhasa when the Chinese invaded Tibet in February 1910. The Indian government gave him refuge in Darjeeling, where, forty years earlier, Nina Mazuchelli had fallen in love with the mountains. On her journey through the foothills to see the Dalai

Lama Alexandra felt as if she had been transported back to the Middle Ages. The steep hills were terraced with narrow green fields and the houses were made of clay, a darker orange than the earth. People worked and dressed as they had for centuries. At Kalimpong, twenty miles from Darjeeling, a colorful mixture of tribal people thronged the streets: tall handsome Khams from eastern Tibet, round-faced smiling Sikkimese, Tibetan women in long, brightly-striped skirts, Nepalese traders, Bengali merchants, a few mysterious Chinese, and some of the red-robed entourage of the Dalai Lama. Kalimpong was the terminus of the mule-train caravans from Tibet. On a fine day the snowy peaks of Everest and Kanchenjunga could be seen. There was a briskness and freshness in the air, deliciously invigorating after the hot plains.

Alexandra was the first Western woman ever granted a private audience with the Dalai Lama. He was so impressed with her knowledge of Buddhist doctrine that his final words to her were, "Learn the Tibetan language!" To Alexandra it was a portentous command.

Here in the Himalayan foothills Alexandra also met Sidkeong Tulka, the Crown Prince of Sikkim. Sidkeong Tulka was a lama[4] as well as a prince and Alexandra questioned him eagerly about Lamaism, as this ancient branch of Tibetan Buddism is often called. The young Prince had been educated at Oxford and spoke English more fluently than his native tongue. She felt fortunate indeed to be introduced to Tibetan Buddhism by such a man. He graciously invited her to Gangtok, the capital of Sikkim, to acquaint herself further with Lamaism. Thinking what a good article she could write for the *Annales du Musée Guimet*, Alexandra rode off to Sikkim. It was a journey of several days by horseback through dense rain forests filled with exquisite tree orchids, brightly colored birds and rare butterflies; then up a treacherously steep switchback trail where the slate mountains often gave way in catastrophic landslides. Her pony slipped and slid so much that she scarcely stayed mounted. She understood then why everyone insisted she ride astride as all women did in the mountains from Darjeeling to Gangtok.

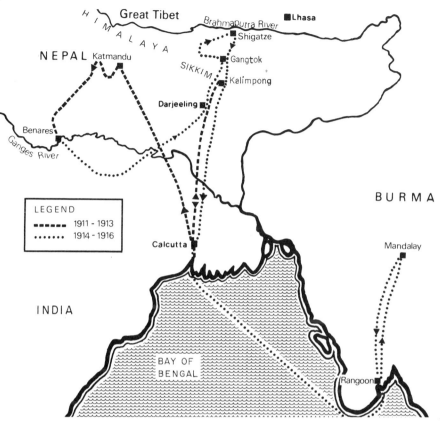

In his father's gardens at Gangtok, Sidkeong Tulka had built his home on the model of an English country house with touches of Tibetan decoration at the windows and eaves. There Alexandra, the Prince and his chaplain, a lama of the Red Hat sect, whiled away long afternoons discussing the mysteries of Tibetan Buddhism —the distinctions between the unreformed Red Hats and the Dalai Lama's Yellow Hats (so named because of the colors of their ceremonial headdress), the phenomena of clairvoyance and levitation, and the all-important Tibetan death rituals. The Prince, dressed in heavy brocade robes, sat on a couch; Alexandra and the lama were in armchairs. Beside them were small gaily painted tables to hold their tea bowls, which were Chinese porcelain with silver saucers and pagoda-shaped covers studded with coral and turquoise. Dawasandup, an interpreter the Prince assigned to travel

147

in Sikkim with Alexandra, sat cross-legged on the floor at their feet. Thus was rank observed. Alexandra, an outsider and a woman, was given deferential status. Their bowls were continuously replenished with tea from a large silver teapot brought round by a young attendant. Incense perfumed the air. Drifting down from the Royal Temple higher on the hill was the faint drone of lamas chanting.

How far it all was from the Sorbonne, where, Alexandra reminded Philippe in a letter, some men tormented poor women who tried to learn something in order to earn their daily bread by means other than sex. Those misogynists, she said, tried to trip women on the corkscrew staircases, kicked them, and squeezed them between the doors and walls. Several times the police had to be called in to protect the women students. It was a torment Philippe could not understand. He may even have laughed—as a man how could he comprehend the milieu of women?

Alexandra lingered on in Sikkim. She visited villages and monasteries with the Prince. The rustic pomp of the tiny court, traveling much in the manner of a medieval court riding circuit, was, she said, like a dream of a very old world. The Prince encouraged her to exhort the monks to practice a purer Buddhism and Alexandra took to the task with zeal, lecturing at the monasteries on the pure doctrine. In June 1912, the Dalai Lama was able to return to Tibet: the Manchu Dynasty had fallen in China and the Chinese troops in Lhasa mutinied. Alexandra went to bid him farewell at the Jelep Pass twenty-five miles from Gangtok. The spiritual leader of Tibetan Buddhism, in his sedan chair with his enormous colorful entourage on mule-back, wound his way over the pass and into the mountains, returning triumphant to his Holy See, Lhasa.

Alexandra spent the rest of the summer in Sikkim. In October she visited the monastery of Pemionchi (or Pemayangtze) where Nina Mazuchelli had been so enchanted by the lamas' services. In November she went to Nepal, then returned to India and rented a small apartment from the Theosophical Society in Benares to resume her journalism and the study of Hindu philosophy. She was content with her arrangements when suddenly everything seemed to go awry: she felt ill and had hallucinations; hostile forces seemed to conspire against her. Whether it was fever or fatigue she did not know. Then, like a deliverance, Sidkeong Tulka offered her an apartment in the monastery of Podang situated in the fog-shrouded forests about ten miles from Gangtok. She accepted with alacrity.

Back in the Himalayan foothills her spirits were soon restored. She found a tutor to instruct her in Tibetan. She wrote Philippe that at her age (forty-four) she must not delay learning the language. She reminded him that she was in a singular position as a woman and a militant practicing Buddhist. Orientalists in the West would be severely critical of her writing. She wanted above all to be completely accurate and document her findings thoroughly so that she could return home "a person of some importance in the world of Orientalists." What she needed was a bit more time and experience. "Don't you think, Mouchy," she wrote, "that given our situation and our characters we can make the sacrifice to be separated a little longer?" Her hope was to spend a little time in Tibet if the authorities would let her. Then she would leave India and travel home via Japan, with her cycle of studies on Buddhism in northern Asia completed.

Alexandra did not wheedle Philippe for money and she assured him continually that she would return home if he wished. She did not want him to be miserable, alone in Tunis, and she was grateful for his support—"you know, Mouchy, I love you very much for what you have done."

But Philippe's patience must have been sorely tried by her reluctance to leave Asia. On December 7, 1913, she answered him in a sterner tone: "I know you make sacrifices to provide me with a life that displeases you." Earlier she had told him how the lamas of Sikkim had conferred on her the designation of a "lamina (*lama femme*)," and given her a lama's red robe to wear. Philippe chided her for wanting adulation, for playing at being a saint—a charge she hotly denied.

In February 1914, the Crown Prince's father died and Sidkeong Tulka became the Chogyal or ruler of Sikkim. As the head of state

Alexandra's camp in the Himalayas.

he was compelled to spend most of his time in Gangtok so Alexandra traveled alone from Podang to remote monasteries, taking with her only Dawasandup, the interpreter, and several porters to carry her camping gear through the azalea and rhododendron forests, and up and down the nearly vertical hills. She made a trip to the north where Sikkim borders Tibet. It was one of her most memorable journeys, as she recalled in *Magic and Mystery in Tibet*:

> A few miles farther, the fairy-like gardens gradually grew thin and scattered, till a few rosy patches only remained here and there, where dwarf bunches of azaleas struggled obstinately for life against the dizzy heights.
>
> The track now entered the fantastic region near the frontier passes. In the intense silence of these wild majestic solitudes, icy, crystalline purling brooks chatted gently. From the shore of a melancholy lake, a golden-crowned bird solemnly watched my caravan as it passed.

Up and up we went, skirting glaciers, catching
occasional glimpses of crossing valleys filled by huge
clouds. And then, without any transition, as we issued from
the mists the Tibetan tableland appeared before us,
immense, void and resplendent under the luminous sky of
Central Asia.
Since then I have traveled across the country lying
behind the distant ranges . . . but nothing has ever dimmed
in my mind the memory of my first sight of Tibet.

She returned to Podang monastery and Darwasandup told her
he was going to India. Alexandra asked if she might have a small
boy, not as an ordinary servant or porter, but as a personal attendant. Darwasandup chose a little Sikkimese lad about fifteen years
old named Yongden who had entered a Red Hat monastery at the
age of eight. He singled out Yongden simply because the boy had
expressed a yen to travel: somehow he had heard about the Philip-
pine Islands and wanted to see them.

It was an auspicious choice. From that time forward Yongden
shared all of Alexandra's travels and never left her side until his
death in France at the age of fifty-five years. The relationship
suited perfectly Alexandra's growing tendency toward despotic
benevolence. She was Yongden's teacher, seer, and arbitrator,
though in later years she insisted on his superior knowledge in
certain religious areas and respectfully addressed him as Lama
Yongden. Probably she craved a companion—someone with whom
she could talk about the matters that interested her, a witness to her
achievements, someone to assist and be with her as she grew older.
Yongden satisfied all these needs splendidly. Even though he was
Sikkimese, he had a British passport because he was born in a
British protectorate. He was registered as Arthur-Albert David,
born Mondo, Sikkim, 1899; occupation, Buddhist priest and
explorer.

In August 1914 the First World War broke out in Europe. It
did not seem to Alexandra a propitious time for returning home. A
Sikkimese lama suggested to her that she might cross the border

just a few miles to visit a Tibetan monastery. She knew this was illegal because the permit issued visitors to Sikkim indicated that they could not proceed to Nepal, Bhutan or Tibet without special authorization from the Government of India. To Alexandra this seemed ridiculous. She simply went.

Small as it was, this Tibetan monastery—Chörten Nyima—was infinitely more interesting than the degenerate ones in Sikkim, where she had found most of the lamas to be illiterate and slovenly, and much given to drink. But most surprising to Alexandra was the presence, at the monastery of Chörten Nyima, of four nuns. "Numerous examples of strange contracts are to be seen in Tibet," she wrote, "but what most astonished me was the tranquil courage of the womenfolk. Very few Western women would dare to live in the desert, in groups of four or five or sometimes quite alone. Few would dare under such conditions to undertake journeys that last for months or even years, through solitary mountain regions infested by wild beasts and brigands." Alexandra was intrigued. She learned that communities of fewer than a dozen nuns each were scattered through the rocky heights of Tibet, some of them at such great altitudes they were blocked in by snow as long as six months of the year. Even more astounding, women lived as hermits in caves or traveled as lone pilgrims.

These were ways of life for women that Alexandra had never dreamed of, and she may have taken their example as a challenge: what a Tibetan woman could do, she could do too. On her return from Tibet she contrived to establish herself as an anchorite in a cave in Sikkim at an elevation of about 13,000 feet.

The Tibetan nuns told Alexandra of a magician *gomchen* or hermit who sent *tormas*, ritual rice cakes, whirling through the air like birds to wreak havoc on those who did not obey his orders. "Oh! to talk with this magician who shot avenging cakes through space! . . . I was dying with desire to meet him." On her first attempt to see the famous hermit she was thrown from her horse and knocked unconscious. Previously she had been riding a yak, which was not bridled, and so she forgot to take up the horse's reins. Her servants knew the fall was an omen that she should not proceed. As she lay

Alexandra David-Neel with Yongden.

recuperating on a cot Yongden huddled trembling in the corner, crying at her rashness. But she persisted.

The hermitage of the *gomchen* was not as stark as Alexandra imagined—a cave of course, but enclosed by a wall of uncemented stones and a solid wooden door, the interior divided by a curtain into a kitchen and a living room furnished with wooden chests and two low tables. The customary offerings were on the small altar: "copper bowls filled with water, grain and butter lamps."

The hermit lama met Alexandra hospitably and offered her buttered tea warmed over a fire lit on the ground of a smaller cave down the mountainside from his. Here she spent her first night alone in what she called a prehistoric dwelling, her blanket laid on the bare rock, her servants and Yongden at some distance in a hut. A bitter breeze blew through cracks in the stone walls. The only sound was the roar of water rushing through the gorge far below. She was afraid to move in the darkness for fear of cutting herself on the jagged rocks. The circumstances appealed enormously to her romantic nature. "I feel that the hermit's life, free of what we call 'the goods and pleasures of the world,' is the most wonderful life of all." After a week or so she persuaded the *gomchen* to accept her "not exactly as a pupil, but on trial as a novice, for a certain time," on the condition that she not return to Gangtok or make any journey until released by him. "The adventure was becoming exciting," she wrote. "The strangeness of it aroused my enthusiasm."

The *gomchen* belonged to the Red Hat sect which does not demand celibacy. He had a wife and a young boy as an attendant. Alexandra's retinue consisted of Yongden and some servants—the exact number she did not indicate, but she justified their employment: "It would have been difficult for me to fetch water and fuel and to carry these burdens up to my cave. Yongden, who had just left school, was no more experienced than I at this kind of work. We could not do without servants to help us, therefore an ample supply of provisions and a store-house was indispensable since we were facing a long winter during which we should remain completely isolated." It would not be a bed of roses, she wrote Philippe, but it would be economical.

Winter came, covering the countryside with sparkling white snow. It piled up, untracked, in the valleys at the foot of the mountain where Alexandra was perched. Her single daily meal was slipped behind a curtain at the entrance to the rough cabin she had added to her cave, and the dishes were taken away by a servant boy she never saw. (A liberating achievement many women of means as modest as David-Neel might envy was that she never learned to cook but always managed to be served.) She studied the Tibetan language and read the lives of famous Tibetan mystics. She talked with the *gomchen* when he periodically broke his solitude, and from him learned to speak Tibetan with a true Lhasan accent. Equally important, she learned from their long talks about the customs and people of Tibet. This tutelage prepared her as no amount of formal study could to enter into and be accepted in Tibetan society.

In January two lamas brought her the mail from Gangtok, including a package from Philippe. It contained a warm dressing gown. Holding the gown close to her Alexandra was stirred by old memories. Tears filled her eyes and for a moment she wept. The cold was fierce. Rhuematism and influenza plagued her. In February snows blocked the trail and she was totally isolated. An extraordinary silence settled over everything.

A bear came looking for food and soon learned to return for bread and other delicacies she threw to him. Snow storms abated and April came. The rhododendrons blossomed far down the mountain. A porter came with letters from Europe written five months earlier. Alexandra knew she could not keep her servants in this lonely retreat any longer. She dreaded returning to civilization but noted sensibly that she had "never let myself be taken in by the illusion that my anchorite's home might become my final harbor." She was still bound by Western ideas of duties and cares. But she had made her "'debut' in the role of anchorite" and Yongden had begun his "apprenticeship as an explorer." She had "tasted the intense voluptuousness of that peculiar life." The memory of that winter of 1914 and '15—utterly without pressures, deadlines or demands from other people, with her own schedule for solitary study and long hikes through the forests—gave her great joy to the end of her life.

It seemed impossible to return immediately to city life: after a winter in the wilderness, even the one street of Gangtok bazaars would be like a bustling metropolis. So Alexandra and Yongden turned north and crossed once more the forbidden but unguarded frontier into Tibet. Alexandra's goal was the famous Tibetan monastery of Tashilhunpo at Shigatze, the seat of the Tashi Lama, or Panchen Lama as he is more frequently called today. The hierarchy of Tibetan Buddhism is headed by the Dalai Lama and the Panchen Lama. Spiritually they are of the same rank but the Dalai Lama, at the time, had superior temporal power.

It was a four-day ride from Chörten Nyima where Alexandra had met the nuns. She left there with Yongden and a monk hired as their servant and guide. All were on horseback, their luggage in great leather saddlebags and a pack-mule carrying two small tents and provisions. Hail pelted them, then snow fell hard and fast until it nearly reached their knees. When they set up camp they were flooded by an overflowing stream. Alexandra spent the night standing on the only spot not covered with icy water.

But she pressed on and at last came in sight of the object of her journey. "In the bluish gloaming, the enormous monastery of Tashilhunpo stood in the distance: a mass of white buildings crowned with golden roofs that reflected the last dim rays of the setting sun." This magnificent Tibetan monastery met all her expectations. She was received by the Tashi Lama and his mother, who invited Alexandra to be her guest. In the great temples, halls and palaces she found "a barbaric splendor"—gold, silver, turquoise and jade in lavish display. The "special psychic atmosphere" of the place captivated her. Hours of talk with the learned monks and lamas led to the bestowal on her by the Tashi Lama of the robe of a graduate lama—"a kind of diploma of Doctor *honoris causa* of the Tashilhunpo university." She went on to Narthan, the largest printing establishment in Tibet, where she found monks sitting on the floor inking engraved wooden blocks and cutting beautiful rice paper, all the while chatting and drinking buttered tea. "What a contrast," she exclaimed, "to the feverish agitation of our newspaper printing rooms."

Alexandra longed to see more of Tibet but she was pulled back to India where her trunks, notes and collection of photographic negatives were stored. How could she have felt those things important? she mused later; how much she had to learn about the insignificance of material possessions. "How great was the mental transformation necessary to enable me to become, a few years later, a joyful tramp in the wilds of Tibet."

In Gangtok Alexandra received a letter informing her that the Government of India had ordered her deportation for "having crossed the Sikkim-Tibetan frontier into Tibet without a pass."[5] She was liable to penalties under the law, which included a fine of 100 rupees for the first offense, 500 rupees for the second, or "to simple or rigorous imprisonment for a term not exceeding three months, or to both." She was given fourteen days to quit Sikkim.

Nothing could have fixed Alexandra's resolve to travel in Tibet more than this notice of deportation waiting for her when she returned to Gangtok. All her rebellious impulses were aroused. "What decided me to go to Lhasa," she wrote, "was, above all, the absurd prohibition which closes Tibet."

Now the only possibility of gaining access to the closed land lay through China. Alexandra and Yongden left India from Calcutta at the end of 1916. They traveled leisurely through Burma, Japan and Korea, staying at Buddhist monasteries and participating to the extent they could in monastery routine. They arrived in Peking October 8, 1917.

Alexandra had heard about the great Kumbum monastery near China's largest lake, the Koko Nor, at an elevation of 10,515 feet in the northeast Tibetan highlands. She wanted to visit it. Money for her journey was a problem but if it was not forthcoming and she did not complete her trip, she assured Philippe she would be content to die in the Tibetan desert. Yongden would be near his own country. He could sell her few possessions and travel on to a monastery. But she must see Tibet once more.

On October 31, 1917, Alexandra wrote Philippe that it was no

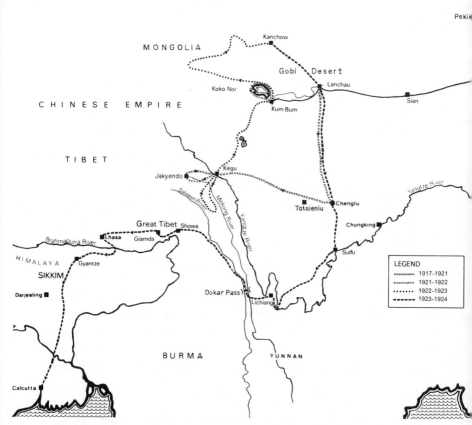

more dangerous to walk in the solitudes of Tibet than to cross the Place de la Concorde. What she craved were great open spaces where she would not feel closed in. There had been too many people in Japan for her. Alexandra had told her husband many times that she was born a savage, a "*solitaire.*" Wild open country did not frighten her.

It would probably have surprised Alexandra to know that the Englishwoman Annie Taylor had handed out cards with Biblical verses to the Tibetans encamped around Kumbum a quarter of a century earlier. Annie spoke Chinese and traveled alone. Alexandra upbraided herself for her lack of the language, but she soon found in Peking a Tibetan lama with whom she could converse. Fortunately he was returning to the region around Koko Nor and she and Yongden joined him and his retinue. Arrangements took time and Alexandra obtained from the French Legation a letter of reference to assist her in obtaining supplies and services en route. The party finally left Peking January 24, 1918, for the far north-western provinces of China.

The interior of China was ravaged by civil wars. Insurgents repeatedly blocked the travelers' route so they had to veer from the Great Silk road south of the Great Wall of China. Several times the lama's little caravan had to seek refuge in a village under fire. During one bombardment, Alexandra reported proudly to Philippe, Yongden was able to overcome his fear and talk calmly with her about things other than the danger at hand.

Difficult as the journey was, Alexandra's happiness increased the farther she moved from the densely populated, well-cultivated coastal regions into the rolling hills and vast grasslands of Central Asia. In Lanchow she declared, "I am in good health and 'high spirits' as the English say." Even an attack by one of her mule drivers failed to upset her. She grabbed her whip and gave him a volley of lashes—unwillingly since she did not believe in violence, but under the circumstances she had to assert her authority in a manner he would understand. From that time on she had no trouble. Her muleteers knew she was not timid. They respected her and obeyed her orders. And she herself bore them no malice: it was the fault of their upbringing, she explained to Philippe, that these ignorant men imagined they could take any woman they wanted.

Travel at the pace of a string of laden mules allows subtle psychological changes to occur in the traveler; it provides time in which to become attuned to an unknown country, to accept more easily the gradual loss of civilized amenities and the increasing simplicity of life. Traveling for days upon end prepares the mind and senses, as jet travel never can, for the sudden thrill when a wondrous sight appears abruptly in a barren landscape.

Alexandra had just such a thrill when, 7 months and 2,000 miles after she had left Peking, she rode up a low ridge and looked down on the great Kumbum monastery. The monastery, established in the sixteenth century, became one of the richest and most important monasteries of Tibetan Buddhism and housed over 3,000 monks. The Abbés Huc and Gabet stopped here for a few weeks in the 1840's. The sight Alexandra beheld was a maze of low buildings growing, as Tibetan architecture seems to, out of the steep slopes of the ravine: golden-roofed temples and flat-topped apartments gleaming with whitewash, a perfect chromatic contrast for the red-robed monks in the narrow streets. Alexandra stayed "in the lulling calm of the monastic citadel" for nearly three years.

Normally women are not allowed to live in a monastery. Alexandra obtained the privilege because of her age, her studies, and "above all powerful protection," by which she meant the blessings of the Dalai Lama and the Tashi Lama. She was assigned a small house "tucked away in the corner of a tiny cloister in the princely palace of Pegyai Tulka." From her balcony she watched the caravans of yaks and camels come and go, heard the bells round their necks ringing gently and saw the pilgrims arriving from all parts of Tibet. In the distance a caravan of black yaks stood out against the white mountains. The sky was an intense blue and there was that distinct clear light of Tibet that she remembered so well.

In a letter to Philippe dated November 11, 1918, Alexandra described the routine of her day at the Kumbum monastery. She rose when the stars were still in the sky and stepped out into the brisk, blood-tingling air on her terrace. At five a.m. the trumpets resounded from the roofs of the temples. At six a boy came in to build a fire in the stove in her apartment and a servant brought tea. Then she dressed and read or walked on her terrace while her room was swept. At nine she was served breakfast. Then she translated and studied ancient Buddhist texts wrapped in iridescent yellow brocade from the Kumbum library. At noon she bathed and worked again at her desk until four, when another meal was brought to her, usually a heavy soup and baked fruit. Afterwards she read and wrote some more and was in bed at nine p.m. She did not mention to "dear Mouchy" her meditations and listening to sacred music.

The comfortable monotony of her days was broken from time

to time when she joined caravans for excursions out of Kumbum. It was the kind of life that she could continue for a million years without physical or mental fatigue. She would have stayed forever but to do so she had to become a member of the monastery and her sex barred her from this privilege.

Yongden, being a young man and a monk, had greater liberty of action and reported to Alexandra those arcane practices of Tibetan Buddhism she could not witness. She did not record any resentment of this discrimination, perhaps because she felt so much more her own woman at Kumbum than she would have been as Philippe's hostess in Tunisia. Early in their correspondence she had argued that women's financial dependency on their husbands was the chief source of friction in marriage and that wives should be paid for their housework. She knew she could not tolerate being a conventional French housewife. In India she was appalled at the status of women, who could not even eat with their husbands. Everywhere, it seemed, women were in a subordinate position. When she read that the French Senate had decided to consider the question of votes for women she commented to Philippe (February 5, 1919) that French men and women were always at war with each other. There could be no friendships between them as there were among Anglo-Saxon men and women. She had lived in England and met and stayed with Americans in Asia. English and American men had a much more open attitude toward women. Later she considered several times settling in America. But for her at that time Kumbum was a safe haven.

Besides, Alexandra in this period was content to be a student. She found in the East a spiritual serenity that seemed to her totally absent from the West. "Were it not for you, the sole link that remains," she confessed to Philippe, "I would never again set foot in Europe." Her Buddhist philosophy and her friendship with her "dear Mouchy" were, she avowed, the two great strengths of her life.

However, she had great plans that were dependent upon the West. When the war was over she wanted to publish her books there. Although she was fifty-two she was happy to note that the passage of years did not seem to cause a decline in her physical strength. Instead of referring to the autumn of her life as she had done in her forties Alexandra began to consider the long life that probably lay ahead of her. Her father had lived until he was ninety, her mother until she was eighty-seven, and two of her grandfathers had passed their 100th years. If she could live to be 100 years old with a clear mind she would write her books and never be bored. Again and again she thanked Philippe for the money that enabled her to live at Kumbum and make excursions to collect material for her writing. "These years of travel are years of paradise."

In a letter of May 25, 1920, in which she mentioned having recently received news of the end of the war, she told Philippe she wanted to buy a piece of land in the French countryside where they could have a small cottage in a large garden. His pension would be devalued by the terrible inflation in the aftermath of the war, she said, and urged him to consider the wisdom of raising vegetables and rice on their own rent-free land. ". . . When I think of myself I think also of you." Her ties to both Philippe and France were still stronger than she seemed to realize.

She also began to think about taking Yongden, or Aphur as she called him in her letters, home to France. From Alexandra's point of view it made great sense. Yongden had served her for many years without wages, and in a way she served as a mother to him. He could cook and sew a little and be a secretary for her. When they returned to France he could arrange her library and her collection of Tibetan curios, and could assist with her translations of Oriental texts. To recommend him further to Philippe she added that he did not smoke or drink wine. But it was the beginning of a long struggle: Philippe was strongly opposed to Alexandra bringing the young Tibetan home with her.

Since Alexandra could not stay at Kumbum she reluctantly left her scholarly life and took up once more the role of traveler. If she could not become a member of the Lamaistic community she would be a lone pilgrim and explorer. It was time to resurrect her vow to reach Lhasa. Wide reading in French and English had familiarized Alexandra with stories of travelers to Tibet. She knew of the few most famous who had reached Lhasa, among them Thomas Manning in 1811, the Abbés Huc and Gabet in 1846 and the British Military Expedition of 1904. She knew also of the experienced explorers who had failed, such as Sven Hedin, Prince Henri d'Orleans, and others generously sponsored and well equipped. Authorities had turned them back or bandits had killed them. Some were defeated by the rugged terrain and extreme weather. Undeterred, Alexandra set out with Yongden to do alone what these hardy men had failed to accomplish.

A strict chronology and exact routing of Alexandra's travels in the next few years is difficult to establish. Where she was, and when, and for how long, were of little importance to her. Friends said she had absolutely no notion of time, explaining this vagueness as a very Oriental trait. A detractor[6] tried to make much of this un-Western attitude but there have been no valid refutations of Alexandra's claims. It would have been infinitely easier to follow her trail if she had made a clear distinction between her travel books and her philosophical, political and sociological works. But her personal experiences and observations were scattered throughout her works in an eye-witness, journalistic manner without the trained journalist's careful record of time and place. Her chameleonic nature defeated consistency: at one moment she was the bold and daring explorer, at another the spiritual seeker seduced by the contemplative life. Always present in her character, however, was a certain sustaining shrewdness. That shrewdness, coupled perhaps with a French feeling for style, enabled her to create and build upon her own legend—that of a woman alone, joyful and free.

When, after several years in Asia, Alexandra first assumed the role of an independent Buddhist ascetic, she had written to Philippe explaining that her decision demanded a renunciation of the physical pleasures of the world. However, she made it clear that her rejection was completely different from the renunciation of the Christian monk or of the mystic burning to unite himself with his god. "The 'renunciation' of the monk has the character of a sacrifice, while he who dons the robe of the sannyasin does it because he feels aversion, repugnance, for that which the great mass of men regard as the 'good things' and the 'joys' of the world," she wrote in *Buddhism: Its Doctrines and Methods*. "In the words once used by a sannyasin while talking to me, 'he rejects them with satisfaction, as one would feel contentment in throwing off dirty and ragged clothing.' Sannyasa is not a 'means' which one uses to attain an object; sannyasa is an end in itself, a joyous liberation. Moreover, the sannyasin is always freed from social and religious laws; freed from all bonds, he walks on a path which is known to him alone, and is responsible only to himself. He is, par excellence, an 'outsider.'"

From childhood Alexandra had felt herself different, not to be judged by conventional standards, fitting nowhere. Becoming a Buddhist ascetic conferred status and acceptance on her outsider's role. Eliminating sex from her life may have been a relief. She was in her forties when she chose to live in a society not so overtly stimulated by sexual competition as the West. Alexandra was unwilling, though, to give up entirely the advantages a foreigner sometimes had while traveling in Asia: she would switch from Western dress—American coat and her French gloves—to her robes as a "lady-lama," as it suited her purpose.

Much of the country Alexandra traveled over after she left Kumbum was not accurately mapped. Place names were recorded phonetically according to no standardized system and, even more confusing, were often changed over the years as governments came and went. According to a simplified map she made of her journeys, Alexandra's first major exploration was in 1921 around the great lake Koko Nor. Also in 1921 and into 1922 she went south to Chengtu in Szechwan, then turned west toward Tibet until she was deflected by Chinese soldiers. That excursion ended at Jaykendo, a monastery in Tibet's northern plateau, still under Chinese suzerainty. The next year she traveled north again, into Mongolia and the Gobi Desert.

Alexandra's letters during this time record her terrible battle to survive with little or no money. At one point she told Philippe if she did not receive funds soon she might give up the struggle.

The Chinese civil wars disrupted communications and she was always in danger of being shot. Or she might die of starvation or exposure. She wrote that she did not tell Philippe these things to impress him; most writers over-dramatized their journeys. She simply wanted him to understand why she might not return and to establish how, in the event of her death, Yongden would get a message to him.

True to her resolution not to be melodramatic, Alexandra's books say little about her difficulties. In *Tibetan Journey* she said she was traveling modestly in order not to attract too much attention. She managed to have horses or mules for herself and Yongden, plus several servants and a pack animal or two. Bandits looking for rich booty roamed the thinly populated West China regions where the explorer Dutreuil de Rhins had been killed. A few years after Alexandra explored the area two more Frenchmen, Louis Marteau and Louis Dupont, simply disappeared somewhere around the Koko Nor. In 1946 the French anthropologist and archeologist Dr. André Migot, who spoke Chinese and a number of border dialects, was stripped, robbed and left on his own in the desolate region south of the Koko Nor. His caravan of two coolies was much less conspicuous than Alexandra's party, but her keen instinct for sensing trouble and avoiding confrontation saved her from the fates of her unfortunate countrymen. "I cannot imagine any danger I could not successfully circumvent by my wits alone," she declared.

To trip robbers she strung a rope near the ground across the entrance to her tent. Once she flung back the tent-flap and appeared in her nightgown to order off two suspicious-looking nomads who had entered her camp. Under her gown she carried a pistol which she flourished on a few occasions, but she never fired a shot. Though she was scarcely more than five feet tall she was quite capable of using her riding whip to separate men fighting with knives.

In India and Sikkim travel was greatly facilitated by the occasional dak bungalows, those small, comfortable guest houses built by the British along the fairly well-traveled trails where Alexandra did her apprentice traveling. But the government of

China had no such luxuries. It could scarcely control its vast central Asian regions; even the soldiers garrisoned at check points along the lonely routes were apt to be more rigorous in the pursuit of their own than the government's interest. In China Alexandra did not enjoy the privileged status she had in Sikkim under the protection of the Chogyal.

Once she rode on nearly dropping with fatigue rather than accept shelter in the alcove assigned to the women and children in a Chinese house. "Such promiscuity" appalled her. She carried aspirin, boric acid powder, antiseptic cotton wool and olive oil for dressing wounds—the first-aid kit of a prudent traveler. In her saddle-bags were her camera and photographic equipment, notebooks, compasses, thermometers, papers for a herbarium and other paraphernalia peculiar to the West. There was no possibility of disguise; Alexandra's only hope of passing check-points was to slip by them or outwit their guards. This was difficult. In keeping with the Oriental custom she carried a requisition order from the magistrate of the district just left, requiring the next village or town to provide her with meat, butter, milk, cheese and other provisions, as well as the necessary beasts of burden—horses, mules or yaks— should she need fresh ones. Sometimes she had an escort of two or more soldiers "imposed" on her by the Chinese and she almost always sent her card ahead with a soldier or servant to petition the head man or wealthiest citizen for lodgings when she stayed in a town or village. Often she took shelter at missionary outposts, particularly those of the Roman Catholic Société des Missions étrangères de Paris. News of this European woman who spoke Tibetan, had lived at the Kumbum monastery and now wandered the highlands visiting isolated monasteries and remote hermitages filtered along the trails of the West China border. Repeatedly she was frustrated in her desire to push on to Lhasa. Once when ordered back along the same route she had followed inland she staged a scene, threatening to kill herself rather than retrace her steps. "Give me my revolver," she cried to the alarmed soldiers. "I shall kill myself. Everyone will then believe that you have murdered me and you will suffer the consequences of this crime." Yongden played his part in the pretense. Finally the soldiers pleaded with this fierce little woman to just go away quietly. "Many travelers had been stopped on their way to Lhasa, and accepted failure," she declared. "I would not. I had taken the challenge on the iron bridge [where she had been stopped and turned back] and was now ready to show what a woman can do!"

Her long apprenticeship in Asian life was over. She would cease being Madam Alexandra David-Neel, sometime "lady-lama," and don the disguise of a Tibetan beggar woman, a pilgrim to Lhasa. And so, in her fifty-fifth year, Alexandra, with all the zest of youth, set out on her ultimate rebellion against the "powers that be"—a singular, prodigious and exuberant journey into the forbidden land.

My Journey to Lhasa by Alexandra David-Neel has a style and spirit never excelled in her next twenty books. A review in the *Nation and Athenaeum* declared that "as a narrative of adventure it grips the imagination. . . . The crossing of the wild, unexplored parts of Tibet from Mongolia to British India, by a European lady, establishes a record in the annals of exploration." *The Boston Transcript* found it an "interesting and well-written book," and saw that it was "a labor of love," with Alexandra's views of the Tibetans "sympathetic but not credulous, without bias or dogma." *The New Statesman* asserted that "The lure of Lhasa is not so much the lure of the unknown as of the forbidden," and opined that the challenging of prohibitions "has been human nature, especially feminine human nature, since the beginning of recorded time." Assuredly it was Alexandra's nature. This journey was the secret dream of the lonely girl who read fantasies in Paris and ran away from home.

Inevitably, it had all the elements of a fairy tale. There was the pursuit of a hidden secret through mysterious lands and among strange peoples. The guarded secret was Lhasa, the seat of Tibetan Buddhism; the mysterious lands, China, Mongolia and Tibet; the strange peoples, the Tibetan village folk and the tribal nomads, the dreaded Ubes and the treacherous Pos. Included were all the ingredients of a fantastic adventure: traveling in disguise; mistaken identities; false clues; a faithful companion (Yongden); dangers to Alexandra's life; the sudden appearance of a stranger who knows but does not reveal her identity; miraculous escapes accomplished by cleverness and an almost supernatural good luck; final victory over every obstacle; and her happiness secured.

Alexandra was, of course, the protagonist of this tale but she did not see herself as the princess. There were royal overtones in her role as a person of rank who lived in disguise among the poor and they, thinking her one of them, treated her with simplicity and kindness. But no Prince Charming needed to come to her rescue. She was a perfectly capable woman, as she stated: "All sights, all things which are Lhasa's own beauty and peculiarity, would have to be seen by the lone woman explorer who had the nerve to come to them from afar, the first of her sex."

Alexandra and Yongden began their journey from the Gobi Desert above the Koko Nor in China and traveled south to Lanchou (now Kao Lan) and Chengtu in the province of Szechwan. To avoid suspicion they made a great loop west and south from the direct caravan route between Peking and Lhasa. It took them about seven months before they reached Suifu (now Ipin) and Lichiang in the Yunnan province bordering Burma. The country was fairly well settled and Alexandra traveled in her usual style. On October 23, 1923, she wrote Philippe saying it would be her last letter for a long time. Then she proceeded north from Lichiang to a mission house somewhere up the Mekong River. Under the pretense of going on a short botanical expedition as Westerners often did, she dismissed her servants and set out on foot with Yongden. At about the 27th parallel she slipped off the main route and into her disguise. She darkened her hair with a wet stick of Chinese ink and her face with a mixture of cocoa and crushed charcoal, lengthened her hair with black yak-braids, fastened large looped earrings in her ears, put on a coarse woolen Tibetan robe, took up her pack and was off to the unknown.

Some years before, Alexandra had spent several weeks at the

Jakyendo monastery where she had an apartment next to General George Pereira. Pereira was a famous British explorer who later died of privation in the Anne Machin mountains in northeastern Tibet. They often met for tea at Jakyendo and visited nearby places of interest together. Now as she followed the Mekong River toward the Kha Karpo mountains and the Tibetan frontier, she had hidden in her boots rough copies General Pereira had let her make from his notes and maps. He had alluded to the possibility of accessible passes above the springs of the river Po where one might reach the high Tibetan plateau undetected. It was a wild country as yet unmapped. This was the direction Alexandra took. At the Dokar Pass (14,890 feet) in the Kha Karpo mountain range she and Yongden stole across the Tibetan-Chinese border. For the next five or six hundred miles, between the 97th and 99th parallels, she followed rough tracks no Westerner had trod. She climbed unnamed summits and crossed unexplored rivers. Only the names of the larger villages and monasteries appear on the British and American armies' maps (scale 1:1,000,000), so a detailed tracing of her route is impossible. But whichever way she went the terrain was nearly straight up and down. Most of the numerous passes that had to be crossed ranged between 10,000 and 15,000 feet, but a 17,000- or 18,000-foot elevation was not uncommon. Alexandra guessed that the highest summit she climbed was about 19,000 feet. She may have crossed the Yoko Pass, which is still unmeasured, over a 21,700-foot mountain, still unnamed, west of the Salween River. Snowstorms nearly buried her and Yongden. Once they went without food or water for thirty-six hours. And they tramped as long as nineteen hours straight. But from Alexandra's description in her book, it was more a romp than a slog.

"The scenery was grand beyond all description," she enthused. The snows on the passes were an "overpowering spectacle" that moved her deeply. She and Yongden trudged on until two in the morning beneath a beautiful moon and she did not feel tired, only sleepy. All nature and its creatures took on a romantic hue. Once she perceived three well-dressed Tibetan men coming toward her across the fields. To her they seemed like handsome medieval knights, with long hair falling freely to their shoulders, fur robes and vests of red and green. At their waists were short swords with jeweled sheaths. Seeing them set in the "mystic landscape," Alexandra was reminded of paintings by Hans Memling which she had seen in her youth.

Like Sir Richard Burton, the famous Victorian traveler and linguist, Alexandra adopted the role of a pilgrim. Burton made his celebrated trip to Mecca in the disguise of a Muslim from India. Alexandra passed as a Tibetan peasant woman traveling with her lama son on a long devotional pilgrimage to Lhasa. As she and Yongdon came closer to Lhasa she changed her identity slightly by donning a different hat and altering her story so that she would always appear to be from a region most remote from her present company's direct experience. There was constantly the danger of detection. A gesture, a mis-pronounced word, a gap in her knowledge could give her away in an instant. But, like a consummate actress, she lived the role she played: "I felt myself a simple *dokpa* of the Koko Nor," she said. "I chatted with the women about my imaginary black tent in the Desert of Grass, my cattle, and the feast days. . . . I knew by heart the region I described, for I had lived there long."

Alexandra's canteen while she was traveling in disguise consisted of an aluminium pot, a bowl, a spoon, and a Chinese traveling case containing one long knife and a pair of chop-sticks which she hung from her belt.[7] In her pack was a small white tent which she seldom dared to pitch unless she was far from villages or shepherds' camps, but which she often used as a cover to hide under. If she and Yongden could find a hollow in the earth about the size for them to crawl into with their packs, they would stretch the tent across it and strew a few leaves and twigs on it for camouflage so it passed as a patch of snow. Often at night the weight of her money belt and revolver on her breast kept her from sleep. Once when she was about to be carried across a river on a man's back she quickly pretended to be looking for lice in her gown in order to shift the money bag under her left armpit and the revolver under her right. But as always she relied on the "'winged words' of the Goddess Juno" rather than a gun. With her iron-spiked staff she held off the vicious guard dogs at Tibetan houses where she and Yongden occasionally sought shelter. Unrestrained, she entered completely into the life of the poorest peasant—dipping her unwashed fingers in the communal soup bowl, accepting scraps of meat from a generous woman who cut them on the lap of her dress "which had been used, maybe for years, as a handkerchief and a kitchen towel." She carried a small leather bag, greasy and black with dirt. In it was a piece of dry bacon, some *tsampa* (the local barley flour), a little salt and a brick of tea. When she and Yongden fixed a meal for themselves, it was a soup made from tiny bits of the bacon and a few pinches of *tsampa* thrown in boiling water, followed by tea with salt and a little butter if they were lucky enough to have some. It was worlds away from the French cooking she remembered. "My father's dogs would not have eaten such a thing," she told Yongden with a laugh, but assured him that, considering the circumstances, their soup was delicious. And in any case, wretched food was the least of her trials. "In a country where everything is done in public, down to the most intimate personal acts," she wrote, "I was forced to affect peculiar local customs which embarrassed me terribly. However, our way at times lay through large tracks of uninhabited land, and the greater freedom I enjoyed there somewhat relieved my painful tension."

To travel as a peasant was a rude change from the days when she was given a private room, wore her beautiful lama robes and was invited to bless people, cure the sick and make prophecies. Now Yongden, as a red-robed lama in his mid-twenties, traveling with his aged mother, was the one asked into the houses to officiate, while Alexandra washed the bowls in the stream or sat at a dusty doorstep chanting the Buddhist prayer, *Aum mani padme hum!*— Oh Jewel in the Lotus! She became rather expert, she said, and was complimented "for the nice way I had of chanting it." The success of her masquerade pleased her enormously. She firmly believed that living among the people was the only way to observe and understand their lives—a surprisingly modern view seldom held by Western travelers in her time, who were generally so confident of their superiority that the psychological distance between them and the people they traveled among was unbridgeable.

Understandably though, Alexandra preferred the uninhibited country where she could sleep under a tree in a "sylvan glen," or in a cave. It was easier for the world to seem enchanted in the wilderness. A heroic tone crept into some of Alexandra's accounts of her and Yongden's feats, but none of the solemnity or terrible grappling with one's will to persevere that is evident in many books of exploration. When conditions were worst in her "phantasmagoric land of heights," Alexandra looked back down the mountain at the tiny figure of Yongden laboring up the glacier's edge and her heart was moved with compassion. "I would find the pass; it was my duty; I knew that I would!" When she was numb to all sensation, tearing her hands and face on the thorny bushes, she lumbered on, "hypnotized by the will to succeed." When afraid of being found out by officials, she was resolute: "Not for one minute did I consider the idea of giving up the game. I had sworn that a woman could pass, and I *would!*"

But for most of the journey she felt that to "the one who knows how to look and feel, every moment of this free wandering life is an enchantment." She knew that an epicure lurked in her ascetic heart; that privations enhanced pleasure; that it was a voluptuous thrill to sleep in a shepherd's hut with a wood fire burning only if one had slept first in a cold earthen cave.

One particular night Alexandra and Yongden tramped for nineteen hours, much of it through snow over a mountain pass—an astounding feat of courage and endurance for a fifty-six-year-old woman. But an even more amazing phenomenon occurred that moonlit night. When they halted at the edge of the snow line, too exhausted to go on, Yongden made a terrifying discovery: the flint and steel he carried were wet. There was no other way for them to light a fire; if they stopped to rest without a fire they would freeze. Yongden felt strong enough to wave his arms and stamp his feet to keep his blood circulating, but he saw that Alexandra could not maintain such vigorous exercise until the sun rose. Desperately he pleaded with her to attempt the ancient art of *thumo reskiang*, the willed creation of internal heat. She knew it, he reminded her.

I had inured myself, during five months of the cold season, to wearing the single thin cotton garment of the students at a 13,000-foot level. But the experience once over, I felt that a further training would have been a waste of time for me, who, as a rule, could choose my dwelling in less severe climates or provide myself with heating apparatus. I had, therefore, returned to fires and warm clothes, and thus could not be taken for an adept in the *thumo reskiang,* as my companion believed! Nevertheless, I liked at times to remember the lesson I had learned and to sit on some snowy summit in my thin dress of *reskiang.*[8]

Yongden, seeing his adopted mother sitting trance-like in her meditations, must have assumed she was seeking the appropriate attitude to practice this arcane art. He wandered off to collect dried cow dung and dry twigs more to move about than with any hope that they could be kindled.

Deep in her reminiscences, Alexandra remembered that she too had dried dripping sheets wrapped round her when she was a student of *thumo reskiang.* Why then, couldn't she dry the flint and steel in the same way? *Thumo reskiang* had nothing to do with religion; it was merely a way that Tibetan hermits had devised of coping with the rigors of living ascetically in the cold heights of Central Asia. Therefore, using the art for a mundane purpose showed no lack of reverence.

Alexandra tucked the flint and steel and a pinch of moss under her robe and began to concentrate in the prescribed ritualistic manner. She saw flames rise all round her, higher and higher, their tongues curling above her head. She felt "deliciously comfortable," and all sense of time left her.

Suddenly a loud crash broke her concentration. It was the ice breaking in the river. The flames died down as if disappearing into the earth. Alexandra opened her eyes. A chill wind blew but her body burned. Quickly she gathered a little dry grass and dried cow

Monastery of Potala.

dung. She felt the fire bursting out of her head and fingers. Half-conscious, she knocked the flint against the steel and a single spark sprang up. Then another. The grass caught fire. The flames leaped higher and higher as she fed them. When Yongden returned he was astonished:

"How have you done it?" he asked.

"Well, it is the fire of *thumo*," I answered, smiling.

The lama looked at me.

"True," he said. "Your face is quite red and your eyes are so bright. . . ."

"Yes," I replied, "that is all right. Let me alone now, and make a good buttered tea quickly. I need a very hot drink."

I feared a little for the morrow, but I awakened in perfect health when the sun touched the thin cloth of our tent.

The last dreaded hurdle was at Giamdo Dzong. Here they

joined the China Road, the great caravan trail, for the last 400 miles to Lhasa. There was a toll bridge to cross at Giamdo and all travelers to Lhasa had to obtain passes. Alexandra and Yongden repeatedly discussed how they would surmount this final obstacle. But when the time came the problem disappeared. How often this happened on one's travels, Alexandra observed. When Yongden went into the officials' house at the check-point to petition for the passes, she sat on a stone at the door and chanted her prayers. No one paid the slightest attention to her.

Lhasa is situated on a grassless plain in a 11,830-foot-high valley ringed by dark, brown hills. A short distance from it is the magnificent Potala, the fortress palace of the Dalai Lama. The Potala rises like a preternatural growth from a large hill of rock in the middle of the valley floor, its sheer walls enclosing hundreds of rooms, a bewildering complex of stairs and a labyrinth of passages. Crowning it are the golden-roofed Chinese pavilions, visible for miles around. These golden roofs catch the eyes first. The great Potala dominates the imagination of all who long to see Lhasa.[9]

But the day Alexandra approached Lhasa it was hidden by a fierce sandstorm blowing across the plain. Undismayed, she interpreted the storm as a propitious omen helping conceal her entrance to the sacred city. Fortunately, it was the time of the New Year's festival in February, and Alexandra and Yongden joined the multitudes of pilgrims flocking to the mecca of Tibetan Buddhism for the month-long pagentry of religious ceremonies and general merrymaking. She had seen many of the ceremonies before, but always as a foreigner whose servants made way for her through the crowd. Now she was one of the crowd and delighted in it, gleefully noting that she was so short she escaped the blows of the soldiers holding back the rabble. Caught up in the jollity, she sat on the walls with the motley mobs and watched the religious processions, the masked lama dances and the horse races. She ate at the bazaar stands, became involved in the arguments and intrigues of her fellow lodgers at the humble inn, bargained for cheap wares, surreptitiously bought books and had a marvelous time.

But the Potala was her ultimate goal. She tested her disguise by bold ventures into tea houses and the main bazaar, and was mistaken for a Ladaki from western Tibet. With little difficulty she assumed the manner of a stubborn peasant woman a bit confused by the local customs but set on getting what she wanted. To cover her entrance into the Potala, where pilgrims were allowed during the New Year festivities, Yongden accosted two simple Tibetan villagers who had come to the capital to sell barley. He offered to show them through the Potala. By seeing the shrines they would achieve great merit. The peasants were delighted to be shown about by a lama. As Alexandra described it: "The three men walked in first, strong in the superiority of their sex." She followed—an old woman unworthy of notice.

The Potala was not a disappointment. Solid gold butter lamps stood on every altar. There were enormous images everywhere of the Buddha and all his incarnates, either in gold or silver, or sometimes copper. One large silver image had eleven heads and another a thousand hands, each with an eye engraved in its palm. Every shrine room was festooned with silk religious banners in the five mystic colors, white, green, red, blue and yellow. In room after room were gifts from the Chinese emperors—priceless porcelains and exquisite carvings of jade in all colors. There was a surfeit of riches to satisfy the most extravagant expectations. Alexandra read the pictures depicting the legends of gods and saintly men painted on the walls of the galleries and corridors. She recognized in the dark recesses the images of aboriginal gods and demons, denizens of the animistic world of the Bön religion that prevailed before Buddhism. From the roof of the Potala she enjoyed the view of Lhasa spread on the plain below—and she ruminated on how she would have felt ashamed if, at the end of so arduous a journey, she had been able to catch only a brief glance of the exterior of the famous citadel. Instead, her victory was complete.

After two months Alexandra left Lhasa quietly, traveling by horseback with Yongden and one servant. She had changed to the dress of a lower-middle-class woman, secure in the knowledge that officials had little interest in those leaving the capital. The horses were necessary because she had bought so many books to add to her collection and wanted to find still more at monasteries along the way to India. She chose to return via British India to show the government that they could not interfere with her (and everyone's) natural right to travel where they chose, unrestricted by the false boundaries of powerful countries.

Mr. David Macdonald, the British Trade Agent in Gyantze, the last town in southern Tibet before entering Sikkim, wrote about Alexandra's arrival there in his book *Twenty Years in Tibet*. One day his servant announced that a woman, dressed in a white Tibetan robe and accompanied by a lama, insisted on speaking to him. "She spoke very tersely," said the servant, "just like a European." Thinking his daughter was playing a practical joke on him, Mr. Macdonald asked her to be shown into his bedroom. He feigned sleep for a while and then, without looking up, told her to leave and not be silly. To his astonishment the woman informed him that she was Madame Neel. He immediately jumped to his feet and ushered her into the sitting room for tea. She told him where she had come from. Her journey from China to Tibet "was a wonderful feat for a woman of her age and physique," Mr. Macdonald said, particularly since "She appeared very frail, and to succeed as she had called for immense courage and vitality." No doubt she had "undergone incredible hardships," he wrote, for "as a beggar, the houses of the better-class Tibetans, where *bona fide* travelers frequently find some hospitality, were closed to her." Macdonald felt it was unfortunate that she had adopted the disguise since it meant she "saw Tibet only from the viewpoint of a poor pilgrim." He noted that she was French but spoke English very well, and "Tibetan like a native."[10]

Alexandra received permission from Mr. Macdonald to stay in the resthouse. His daughter gave her some European clothes to wear on to Calcutta but Alexandra kept her Tibetan garb to dress in for the studio photographer on Chowringhee Street. She would tell Mr. Macdonald very little about her adventures, stating frankly that she preferred to refrain from discussion until after she published her book. But she took the precaution of having him verify the authenticity of her remarkable journey. The evidence is a document handwritten in ink on plain stationery. It reads:

> To all Whom it May Concern
>   This is to certify that Madame Alexandra David-Neel
> visited at Gyantze while she came through Lhasa from
> Eastern Tibet.
>
> D. Macdonald 21/8/24
British Trade Agent
Yatung, Tibet

Only to Philippe did Alexandra confess that her journey was pure madness. She had been a skeleton when she reached Lhasa, with nothing but skin covering her bones. Then both she and Yongden were stricken with high fevers. The venture had been risky enough for a strong young man like Yongden, but for a woman of her age it was foolhardy. Looking back she had a shiver of fear realizing how often she had not known where she was. But some sense of pride made Alexandra keep these details from her readers. She emphasized the joy and excitement, not the danger and hardship of her adventure.

The purpose of Alexandra's journey to Lhasa was to investigate the practice as well as the philosophy of Buddhism so that her books would be based on observed facts as well as theoretical speculation. She had not gone on a mystical quest for herself. Some time later she was to object to Philippe's impression that her journeys were inspired by religiosity. "I was inspired by the desire to do something no one else had and to try myself physically and intellectually." With great daring and imagination Alexandra had made herself an expert in an area where she was unlikely to be challenged. Hers would be the most authoritative account of Tibetan Buddhism; from her intimate association with Tibetan life she could explain many so-called mysteries.

She probed beyond symbolic figures of speech to understand that the Tibetans recognized the power of the unconscious in much the manner Westerners were just beginning to discover. The imaginary world was recognized by learned lamas to be a powerful force closely intermingled with the conscious world. Exercises of the imagination were part of the initiates' training. The Masters taught that in sleep conventional restraints were abandoned and the real character of the individual acted out his deepest impulses. Therefore dreams were important, but a person must first try to discover how far the immediate waking state influenced the dreamer's consciousness. Most Tibetans believed in premonitory dreams, but not the learned lamas, according to Alexandra.

Time after time she witnessed examples of the power of concentration. She saw it used with great effect to lessen pain and developed to such a high degree among some mystics that it became an anaesthetic, totally obliterating all feeling. She outlined the exercises aimed at producing *thumo*, as she had done on that cold Tibetan night.

Always eager and open to experience, Alexandra wanted to see everything, be in on all the secrets and know all the answers. It was not in her nature to accept anything on faith. It appealed to her sense of superiority that only the elite, the most intelligent, were allowed to hear the secret teachings of Tibetan Buddhism. She had been deemed worthy by a Master and learned from him the theories and precepts of doctrines that had never been written, but were preserved by word of mouth, passing over the centuries from teacher to student. The Master gave Alexandra permission to write down the secret doctrines, but he told her it would be a waste of effort because the mass of mankind was crassly ignorant and would not exert itself to learn. His role was merely that of a questioner who goaded her "to think, to doubt, to seek." The only truth of any value was the truth she would discover herself.

One of the most widespread beliefs in Tibet was that of reincarnation, but Alexandra reported that the intelligentsia did not believe this in a simplistic, literal way. The philosophical theory was based on a belief in an energy formed by all living beings, set in motion by their actions and producing concrete effects. This energy takes various shapes and will continue indefinitely, for "there is no death." But the stories depicting the soul of a dead person looking for an appropriate child to take up residence in are legion and will continue, for as Alexandra commented, "they keep alive the childish thirst for the marvelous among the masses." Yet she was not entirely scornful of simple beliefs. Once, in eastern Tibet, when Alexandra was wearing her "lady-lama" robes, a woman whose father recently had died anxiously asked if he were reborn or still wandering in search of a new body to inhabit. "My ideas on the subject differed greatly from hers," Alexandra wrote, but "I did not feel at all inclined to treat the matter lightly. A daughter's sorrow at the loss of a beloved father is not unknown to me. I myself had too poignantly experienced the bitterness of it to ridicule in another the strange fantasies it can induce." So she assured the woman her father was out of *bardo*, that state between death and birth, and living happily in China where Buddhism was practiced.

Divination was an important part of every Tibetan's life, as Robert B. Ekvall, an American expert on Tibetan culture, who for many years lived in Tibet, ascertained. But interpretation of its significance varied widely. Ekvall noted that L. A. Waddell, the British authority, stigmatized the practice as evidence of a culture ridden with fear and superstition. The Italian explorer and Tibetan specialist Giuseppe Tucci felt it was a wise and valuable recourse to a "deep sea of primal folk wisdom," perhaps more profound than Western science. But Alexandra David-Neel interpreted divination simply and sympathetically; she saw the practice of *mo*, or reading the future, as a helpful device to relieve the hazardous and sometimes fearful burden of decision-making. Divination, in her view, "gave direction to the person seeking it and, by shifting responsibility from him to the oracle, facilitated action."

Alexandra and Yongden were often petitioned to perform *mo*, a ritual that included reciting certain sacred formulae, counting beads on the rosary, and sometimes tossing pebbles in the air, then "reading" their arrangement on the ground. Yongden was very gifted for this ritualistic work, Alexandra claimed, though he had no more faith in it than an Oxford don. Sometimes it was a risky business, particularly when Alexandra was traveling in disguise and successful prophecy was essential to establish Yongden's credibility as a lama. When a persistent and rather unpleasant farmer insisted that Yongden tell him where to find his lost cow, Yongden gave a complicated prophesy concluding with: "everything depends on your cleverness." As Alexandra observed, "A prophet should never be too precise."

In their roles as lamas, Alexandra and Yongden spread enlightenment regarding hygiene and the salutary results of compassion. They told the parents of a girl with swollen legs to bathe and elevate them, and give her several days' rest, warning that none of them would survive their pilgrimage if the girl did not recover. To a couple relentlessly beating a goat they made the solemn disclosure that the goat was an incarnate of a very important person, so it would behoove them to desist lest his relatives take vengeance. And to a pilgrim with an overloaded, exhausted donkey, they warned it would be a bad omen indeed if the donkey died.

Alexandra was not above exploiting the Tibetans' credulity to her own advantage. In her service when she was traveling around the Koko Nor was a young Tibetan who had worked for foreigners before, and who proved his superior knowledge by playing the skeptic at the expense of the other servants whenever he could. One day when Alexandra was returning from bathing in the Koko Nor, she saw the young man, named Tsering, hastily departing from Yongden's tent and stuffing something in his breast pocket. Later Yongden told Alexandra that he had been called from his tent, that he had foolishly left his purse behind, and on his return found three rupees missing. Alexandra did not mention seeing Tsering, but bided her time. Several days later she placed her camp table in front of her tent, arranged a few blades of grass, some grains of rice and a bowl of water on it. She waited until the servants were in their tents prepared for bed, at which time it was the custom to put their valuable possessions, especially money, under whatever served as their pillows. It was a bright starry night. Alexandra sat down before her table, lit some incense, rang the ritual Tibetan bell, beat a tamborine, and chanted some prayers. After a bit she called Tsering and told him in a stern voice that she had seen Yongden's three rupees under his pillow. He was to fetch them at once. Tsering bowed three times at her feet, ran to get the money, and returned, trembling and fearful of the powerful deity in whose power Alexandra had invoked clairvoyance. Alexandra assured the chastened young man that she would protect his life if he reformed. Tsering bowed again and went back to his tent. Alexandra sat on in the silent desert night contemplating "on the strength of ancestral faiths in the human mind and on the deep and mysterious side of the farce that had just been enacted."

At times Alexandra simply recorded extraordinary events without explanation, but more often her accounts are infused with that sense of wonder experienced by the first observers of a strange land and customs. Travelers not seeking data to substantiate theories can be spontaneous and candid about their feelings. In certain moods Alexandra admitted she was susceptible to the consecrated atmosphere that Tibetans created in natural spots where gods were believed to dwell. A huge spreading tree, its branches hung with countless paper flags bearing spells to protect the traveler, appealed to her fancy. Seeing poetic religious inscriptions decorating bridges or a flag proclaiming "Joy to all!" at a summit, moved her to express her preference for those markers over the advertisements one would encounter at similar spots in the West. Protracted journeys through the empty deserts of western China and in the lonely mountains ringing Tibet had sensitized this Paris-bred woman to the powerful influence of natural phenomena on the human mind. "I did not altogether disbelieve," she confessed, "in that mysterious world that is so near to those who have lived long in the wilds."

Now in a state of euphoria at the completion of the most dramatic and dangerous of all her journeys in Asia, Alexandra began, in Lhasa, to write Philippe a barrage of instructions. He must inform everyone of importance about her accomplishment, contact magazines and contract with a clipping service so she would know what the newspapers wrote about her. My dreams of repose are over, she told him. Now she would get down to work to repay him and ensure the comfort of their old age. As soon as Alexandra reached India she set about with great speed to publicize herself and capitalize on her extraordinary experiences.

While visiting Sikkim she received a letter from her former professor, Sylvain Levi, urging her to catalogue the books she had collected. Philippe had made the contacts she asked him to. Offers soon began to pour in from magazines and publishing houses. She heard from Macmillan among others, and Dutton & Co. wrote from the United States, asking to see the manuscript of her story. Again the thought of going to America occupied her. Then she received a subsidy from the French government—and a letter from Philippe. It was the first time she had heard from her husband in nearly two years. His last letter had been dated July 22, 1922. Her reply to this latest one was written from the Catholic Mission at Podang, Sikkim, July 10, 1924. She was happy, she said, to know he was well but she craved more news from him. Also she was completely out of money and waiting anxiously for him to send some so she could book passage on a ship to Europe. "I have completed my journeys," she assured him, "and I am coming home."

Apparently Philippe was alarmed. Perhaps he had become accustomed to the thought that Alexandra was so enamored of the East she would never return to France. So much had happened since she left there in 1911. He had lived through the Great War, and the privations he knew were of necessity, not choice as Alexandra's had been. Their experiences were so different that he questioned the wisdom of her returning to the West. How could they, after so long apart, reestablish their intimacy? His house was too small for the 400 books, manuscripts and Tibetan objects she had collected. He definitely did not want the young Tibetan, Yongden, to share his household. Life would be difficult for all of them; perhaps she should try America.

Alexandra answered him from Calcutta October 21, 1924. "I am not stupid, my good friend. I understand. I know you don't want me at Bône" (where Philippe was posted; now Annaba, Algeria). She reminded him that he had questioned the desirability of her returning once before. But she believed she and Yongden could bring happiness and vitality to his old age. Her gratitude and affection for him were unchanged. Difficult as it might be at her age, she would pay him back—she would even sell her books. She was still elated at the sensation she had caused by her journey to Lhasa; the future looked very bright. "We will meet," she wrote Mouchy, "and embrace each other like two old and faithful friends."

Nine days later, on October 30, Alexandra acknowledged and thanked Philippe for the money he sent. Bubbling with plans she started home, but not too hastily. From Benares (January 8, 1925) she reassured him that she understood perfectly why he wanted to remain master of his own house. What she envisioned were two houses set close to each other in a great garden. They could pursue their own schedules—eat, sleep, study and listen to music on their own—and meet only when they wished. She thought they could find a spot for such an arrangement somewhere in the south of France, perhaps near Nice.

Another anxious letter from Philippe was waiting for her in Colombo, Ceylon. Again he suggested she remain in Asia, and again she assured him she would not upset the quiet of his old age. At any rate it was impossible for her to stay abroad. The only place she wished to live was in Tibet and from there she could not correspond with editors. She was determined to repay him and earn her living. She had to be practical. After all, she speculated with keen foresight, she had a long life yet ahead of her—perhaps as long as forty years.

In Bombay Alexandra met the director of the Musée Guimet, the museum that had fired her dreams of the Orient. He asked her to create a Tibetan shrine for the museum. At a grand luncheon for her, the director, the French consul, the Italian commercial attaché and others persuaded Alexandra that she must establish herself in Paris, not America. The *Revue de Paris* cabled her for a story. Sylvain Levi wrote that he was making arrangements for her triumphant arrival.

So after an absence of nearly fourteen years Alexandra chose to return to her country and to her husband. Despite the promise of success awaiting her it was not a wholehearted decision. Life in the West did not appeal to her. She wrote Philippe in her last letter from Asia: "I am a savage. . . . I love only my tent, my horses and the desert."

IV

When Alexandra disembarked at Le Havre in May 1925, after well over a decade in Asia, she was a very different woman from the one Philippe Neel had married in 1904. The opera singer had become a wandering scholar. She had undergone spiritual and physical trials Philippe had never imagined. She was a proficient in Buddhist rituals of which he knew nothing. And she was asking Philippe to sign papers of adoption that would make Lama Yongden the legitimate David-Neel heir. Philippe did sign the papers. But he did not do it willingly.

Alexandra's expectation that Philippe would enthusiastically welcome her with her Tibetan protégé was unrealistic. Their reunion in the railway station at Marseilles was not a complete success. Philippe returned to his post at Bône, Algeria. Several months later (February 7, 1926) Alexandra wrote and chided him for the coldness he had shown her "devoted little companion" at their first meeting. Yongden was proving to be a great success on her lecture tours, she said. He had assisted her in her hazardous adventures and now she was enjoying the fruits of their achievements.

Her unprecedented journey to Lhasa had proved Alexandra's mettle to herself and to the world, and whatever self-doubts she had harbored were dispelled. As Professor Levi planned, she returned to Paris triumphant. Honors and awards were hers and continued to be conferred on her until the end of her life. Among the first was the Médaille d'argent de la Société Royale Belge Géographie, a Chevalier of the Légion d'Honneur, and the exceptional honor of the Grande Médaille d'or from La Société de Géographie, which is given "to a traveler who, by undertaking a journey outstanding both for its scope and for the original nature of its results, makes a significant contribution to the study of geography."

In March 1926 the first of her three-part article, "A Woman's Daring Journey into Tibet," came out in *Asia* magazine; the following year, when she was fifty-nine years old, the book *My Journey to Lhasa* was published. From then on, for more than forty years, she enjoyed the status of a unique authority on Tibet and Tibetan Buddhism. A torrent of books and articles resulted, and translations were made into English, German, Spanish, Czech, Swedish and Annamite. The most successful in English, after the *Journey*, were *With Mystics and Magicians in Tibet,* and *Initiations and Initiates in Tibet,* both published in 1931. The titles were evocative of the supernatural, probably to increase sales, but they were misleading. Alexandra witnessed many strange practices and extraordinary displays of physical control in Tibet, but nothing supernatural. She did not believe in the occult.

Invitations to lecture throughout France, Belgium, England, and Switzerland kept Alexandra traveling. Dr. A. d'Arsonval, a distinguished medical scientist, and Professor at the Collège de France, asked her to speak to his classes. With admiration he wrote: "This Easterner, this complete Tibetan, has remained a Westerner, a disciple of Descartes and of Claude Bernard, practicing the philosophic skepticism of the former which, according to the latter, should be the constant ally of the scientific observer. Unencumbered by any preconceived doctrine or dogma, Madame David-Neel has observed everything in Tibet in a free and impartial spirit."[12] This testimony was at variance with *The Spectator's* reviewer, who felt that she was "describing practices of extreme absurdity. . . . One may be pardoned for being a little dubious about her intellectual credentials. Still if one accepts the authoress as a guide and not a philosopher, if one reads to find out what the Tibetans believe rather than why they should be so ridiculous to believe it, then there is a good deal of interest here. . . ."

This review reflects the sense of superiority many Westerners had. But Alexandra did not go to Tibet to prove to the Europeans that Tibetans were inferior to them. Occasionally she could not refrain from commenting on the "repugnant mysticism" inherent in some practices: she was an orthodox Buddhist who abhorred superstition. But for the most part her outlook was like that of an anthropologist who tries not to pass value judgments on other cultures when recounting their practices. She was in fact the prototype of a modern field anthropologist—widely read on all aspects of Tibetan society, a master of the language and several dialects. She could think, see, feel and act as a Tibetan and consequently achieved the subtle psychological involvement that underlies communication. But she retained the ability to be detached, to step out of the society she investigated. She wanted to find scientific explanations for the phenomena she observed. When she lectured to Dr. d'Arsonval's classes at the Collège de France she said:

Everything that relates, whether closely or more distantly, to psychic phenomena and to the action of psychic forces in general, should be studied just like any other science. There is nothing miraculous or supernatural in them, nothing that should engender or keep alive superstition. Psychic training, rationally and scientifically conducted, could lead to desirable results. That is why the information gained about such training—even though it is practiced empirically and based on theories to which we cannot always give assent—constitutes useful documentary evidence worthy of our attention.

In *Buddhism, Its Doctrines and Its Methods* (1939), Alexandra criticized modern Buddhism as a distortion of the true teachings of Buddha. He taught doubt and constant questioning, not faith. Skepticism led to research and research led to Knowledge, which was the Buddha's goal. But modern practitioners relied, as do most people of all religious persuasions, on unquestioning faith. This was why, she concluded, supersititon continued to cloud the minds of the masses.

Yet under the mantle of her accumulating honors and growing recognition, Alexandra became increasingly opinionated. Intellectually she deplored dogmatism: "To *believe* that one *knows* is the greatest of barriers which prevent *knowledge*. To imagine that one possesses absolute certainty begets a fatal mental stagnation." But in her personal relations she was impatient and domineering. A friend said that she was undoubtedly a genius, but impossible to live with: she would not suffer fools and that category in her opinion included nearly everyone—except Philippe. She continued to write him in a loving and solicitous tone.

Occasionally they argued over money. Less than a year after her return to France Alexandra accused her husband of not letting her buy a house when there was a better exchange rate for her dollar royalties. As a married woman she had to have his signature to purchase property. Philippe's hurt reply, dated March 23, 1927, is one of his few surviving letters. It was not true, he countered, that she could not do anything without his permission. He gave her absolute freedom and continuing assistance for her world travels; it was she who was imperious, ordering him to look after all of her Oriental purchases. True, she needed his signature to adopt the young Yongden—an action he believed unwise from every point of view. Nevertheless, if she remembered correctly, he kept their meeting in Marseilles amicable and acceded immediately to her wishes. He regretted that their legal situation did not allow her complete liberty. Certainly he did not wish to control her actions or put any kind of obstacle in her way. Were their lives not already separate and independent? But such discussion was fruitless. He would send her the 6,000 francs she requested for a year's rent in advance. "Happily I am able to oblige you since I can still work." His health was not too good, he said—the miseries of age were advancing rapidly—but he would carry on. He hoped her work would bring the recompense it deserved.

From Toulon Alexandra replied three days later that Philippe's kindness was an excellent influence on her work. "I thank you from the bottom of my heart." And in the following letter, April 10, 1927, she expressed her joy that they would be in Paris at the same time. For emphasis she underlined, "*You absolutely cannot leave before we have several days together.*"

However, Alexandra did not feel well in Paris. City life did not agree with her. She suffered from fatigue and colitis. Professor d'Arsonval diagnosed the cause as nostalgia for the country and the life she had left. What she needed was silence, solitude and good fresh air—in short, the mountains. So she planned a long walk in the Alps near Nice. The countryside in the south of France appealed to her and there, in 1927, she bought a house on a hill with a wide view of the mountains. It was on the Route de Nice near Digne, a quiet little town nestled by a river and surrounded by the lavender-colored Alps. Alexandra named her house "Samten Dzong"— Fortress of Meditation. Ever-obliging Philippe shipped from Bône the treasures she had sent him for safekeeping from India, Japan, China and Tibet. In her French home she created an Oriental setting. One room was for meditation and study. There were low narrow couches with pillows, a Tibetan altar and *thangkas* (painted scrolls), a figure of Buddha and old books of unbound block-printed rice paper. In the large garden Alexandra planted acacia, chestnuts and lime trees and prepared a vegetable plot. My greatest desire is that you will come and stay as long as possible, she wrote to Philippe in Algeria. The view was very lovely and she would make the house pleasant enough to satisfy the most difficult taste. There were radiators to assure his comfort in winter and if he were bored he could visit the casinos in Nice.

For nearly ten years Alexandra David-Neel made Samten Dzong her home. She worked prodigiously at her writing and traveled only to lecture. Philippe visited her from time to time. Sometimes they strolled across the bridge into Digne where he often stayed at the luxurious Hotel l'Hermitage. But on October 7, 1934, Alexandra wrote that he would find his customary room at Samten Dzong well heated. If his presence in Bône was not absolutely necessary she hoped he might spend the winter or part of it with her and Yongden. She would have written him sooner but she was waiting to hear from Plon, her Paris publisher, about the book he had read part of the last time he was in Digne. The Plon editors were unanimous in their belief that it would be a great success but they wanted her to cut the manuscript to hold down expenses. It would be an enormous effort, she complained to him; she would have to condense, rearrange and write new connecting passages. Then there would be proofs to correct. All of that would take until December at least—which would not be the best time to go to Siberia. (There was a possibility, which never materialized, of her joining an international expedition through Russia across Central Asia.) And her American editors were urging her to come to the United States.

When she had first returned to France Sylvain Levi had encouraged Alexandra to concentrate on a philological study of Tibetan literature to consolidate her position as a scholar. She was flattered by his proposal but she could not afford it. She had to be a financial as well as a critical success. It was a difficult position: the authority of her popular writing depended on her scholarly status. But scholarship took a great deal of time. In May 1934, Alexandra informed Philippe she had just learned that the Italian Orientalist Giuseppe Tucci was translating the same great Tibetan work, *Tsong Khapa,* that she was. It was imperative that she publish before he did. There was, she believed, a certain Tibetan scholar at the Temple of Lamas in Peking who could help her and Yongden with the literary Tibetan language and so expedite her work. She was impatient to be off to China to find the lama.

Alexandra had cultivated her rootlessness too long to remain fixed forever in one spot and the sudden need to find a scholarly lama may have been an excuse to travel again. When she was sixty-eight years old she made arrangements with Philippe and her publishers, packed up Yongden, and on January 9, 1936, left Brussels by le Nord Express to Berlin. She boarded the Trans-Siberian railway in Moscow to cross Russia to Vladivostok, then continued on through Manchuria to West China and the Tibetan region of Kham.

Slipping effortlessly back into her nomadic way of life, Alexandra revisited the Kumbum monastery near the Koko Nor lake where she had spent those three enchanted years. She gave lectures to the Border Research Society[13] at the Union University in Chengtu and to a group at the French consulate in Hanchow. But it was not the same. The men she had known as the Dalai Lama and the Tashi Lama were dead. China was being devastated by the

Japanese army pushing south from Manchuria and food was in short supply. Rheumatism plagued her joints but she continued to make long walks. Once she had written that "The student who has succeeded in understanding that his life is a dream which he himself supplies with agreeable or terrifying scenes, can insure that the dream does not become a nightmare. He can strive to furnish this relative world, his own creation, with things likely to lead to his own well-being, his happiness." It must have required a tremendous effort to keep her dream world intact and the nightmare at bay. Many Europeans who encountered her in this period were riled by her imperious manner. She was a white-haired, strong-minded little woman with a growing reputation for terrible temper displays when things did not go her way.

From a balcony in Chungking Alexandra watched Japanese planes bomb the airport. All foreigners were suspected by the Chinese of being spies. Their former prestige and power vanished and horror stories of Chinese brutality toward Westerners began to circulate. Both Chinese and Western refugees were streaming south. Even if she got to Hong Kong Alexandra did not have enough money to go farther. And if she did where would she go? Then it dawned on her that she and Yongden would be safest in the Tibetan steppes of the West China border.

In a letter of December 30, 1937, Alexandra instructed Philippe to write her care of the Consulat de France at Yunnanfou, Yunnan. Then she headed southwest toward Tibet. Her destination was the frontier town of Tatsienlu (now Kanting) where Annie Taylor had been sent out of Tibet and Isabella Bird Bishop had been advised not to visit. Tibetan was spoken at Tatsienlu so Alexandra hoped not to be taken for a foreigner. It was on the high road to Lhasa and caravans came and went through it. She had never been in the village but she had been within a day's march to the northwest and knew the country well. If necessary she could reach Burma from there. Once again she was in the East chronicling the perils of her journeys for Philippe in the West.

In Chengtu Alexandra, after some difficulty, was able to hire porters and a sedan chair to carry her up the mountains to Tatsienlu.

A storm raged for the entire ten days it took to make the trip. The path was a sea of mud and she had to walk most of the way soaked to the skin. She and Yongden arrived in Tatsienlu July 4, 1938, just three months before her seventieth birthday.

Nothing stopped Alexandra from writing—not travel or temporary lodgings or an apprehensive state of mind. "For sixteen months we have lived like fugitives," she told Philippe October 9, 1938. That year she was working on a Tibetan grammar, a French-Tibetan dictionary and a book, *Sous des Nuées d'Orage*. At Tatsienlu there were several American Seventh Day Adventist missionaries who gave her and Yongden temporary shelter. She reminded Philippe that she was always happiest on the Tibetan frontier, "And it is in the Orient that I am best able to write books that sell." Tatsienlu was high in the mountains. It reminded her of Kumbum—the air was good, it was quiet and she could live cheaply. But she wanted to stay as separate as possible from the missionaries. There were a few Catholics as well as Protestants. Hatred of foreigners increased daily. She kept in touch with the French ambassador in Chengtu, a man she had known a long time, and he advised her to be ready to flee at a moment's notice. But Alexandra planned to stay on the Tibetan frontier as long as she possibly could.

The Japanese bombarded Chungking and communications began to break down. In November 1938 it snowed continuously for fifty hours. No mail could get through to Tatsienlu. It was hard to tell if letters were lost. It had been so long since she heard from Philippe that she was worried. He was imprudent; she knew he would not take care of himself. She was concerned about his health —and how she would get her manuscripts to editors.

All that winter she worked very hard. By September 1939 she wrote Philippe she had finished *Sous des Nuées d'Orage* and began *L'Ouest Barbare de la Grande Chine*. She was not completely satisfied with what she wrote but she was working during difficult times and seldom could write without disconcerting interruptions.

From her little rented house on the outskirts of the village Alexandra watched Chinese troops climbing the path up the mountains to fight the troops of the Tashi Lama. Later, high officials carried in sedan chairs covered with yellow satin passed her door. She wrote on these embroilments with the zest and understanding of an expert. *Asia* magazine referred to her as the French Orientalist. With Europe at war this American magazine was her best market. Now in her mid-seventies, she sent sprightly copy on politics and personalities in China; the Chinese theater and the problems of news censorship; the effect of the Communists and the Kuomintang on Chinese life; the threat of Japanese bombing; and the joy of the people when the United States and Great Britain renounced their doctrine of extraterritoriality in China. But industrious as she was, money was a constant problem. Inflation was worse in China than in France. On December 5, 1940, Philippe wrote her: "I received 20th November, your letter of July 10. The postal situation is slow. I can understand your financial situation only too well. My French capital is blocked." But he arranged to send her a small sum of money through a U.S. bank. And, he said, among all the sad war news there was one bit of information that would make her happy: Plon, her French publisher, had begun publishing again and was reissuing three books, one of which was hers, the hurriedly written *Sous des Nuées D'Orage*.

That was the last transaction Philippe Neel made for his wife and the last letter he wrote her. His niece who had cared for him notified Alexandra that he died in the family home near Ales in the south of France in January 1941. On February 14 Alexandra cabled from Tatsienlu, "I have received the sad news. I am desolated." Her strongest supporter was gone. "I had lost the best of husbands," she said many times afterwards, "and my only friend."

Alexandra's life-long struggle for economic independence made her sympathetic to the problems of women and a keen observer of their role. In a perceptive article, "Women of Tibet" (*Asia*, March 1934), she looked beyond the obvious pattern of male dominance in social relationships and discerned a subtle balance of equality between the sexes. It could be, she speculated, that the Tibetan women's physical stamina, their ability to cope when men were away, and their early dominance in trade, tended to neutralize the effects of their professed belief in their own inferiority. Like the Tibetan women she admired, Alexandra had tremendous endurance and she continued to cope. France was occupied by the Nazis for another four years after Philippe died. By 1944 the Japanese army had pushed so near Tatsienlu that air-raid alarms were sounded. Cold winds blew through the cracks in Alexandra's small house and she did not have the money to buy fuel for a fire. Out of the window she watched bands of refugees straggling past. Finally, in 1944, after nearly six years in Tatsienlu, Alexandra decided there was nothing left to do but join them. She was seventy-six years old but still sturdy and resourceful. From some scraps of rough material she made a French flag to attach to her baggage for whatever protection it might afford her from the anglophobic Chinese. Then she found some emaciated mules, loaded them with her trunks and, walking herself, she and Yongden took the road south in search of the French Military Mission they hoped would fly them out of China. Some days they found no food. At night they were often without shelter. But Alexandra was undaunted by the hardships and apprehensions of refugee life. She remained a formidable presence, still accustomed to ordering people about, Eastern-style. When she found the French Military Mission, probably in Kunming, they capitulated and flew her, Yongden and 400 kilos of baggage out of China to India.

Back at Samten Dzong in Digne after the war, Alexandra managed to re-create her Asian world. Scholars and admirers visited her. Now an octogenarian, she inspired adulation by her plain staying power. She had wondered, after she had gone to Lhasa, if the story of her passage would enter into Tibetan legend to baffle some future historian of folklore. Now she was a living legend, interviewed by reporters who were born long after her epic journey. But she preferred to concentrate on the future. She struck a bargain with the city of Digne: if they would exempt her from taxation she would bequeath to them the royalties from her books. The officials of Digne agreed—she was famous and they were proud of her. When they built a new secondary school they named it after her. Today her name is emblazoned on the school building's exterior.

Alexandra David-Neel at Samten Dzong, eighty-seven years old.

Yongden died in Digne in 1955 at the age of fifty-five. After a few unsuccessful attempts to keep a suitable secretary, Alexandra found Marie-Madeleine Peyronnet, a young French girl from Algeria. "You will be my consolation and my joy," she prophesied correctly to Marie-Madeleine. As Mademoiselle Peyronnet amusingly described it in her book, *Dix Ans Avec Alexandra David-Neel*, it was a shaky beginning. The Oriental peculiarities of Alexandra's household made her queasy—a box with Yongden's ashes saved for eventual immersion in the Ganges River; a Tibetan rosary of 108 beads made of human bones; insects and mice tolerated with equanimity because, as a Buddhist, Alexandra would not disturb any living creature. By now rheumatism forced her to use two canes and she was more irascible than ever. But she was still an enthusiastic teacher and Marie-Madeleine was hungry to learn. Eagerly she filled the role of pupil which Yongden had occupied for so many years.

Age did not diminish Alexandra's enthusiasm for life. In her nineties that chronic urge to travel gripped her again. She proposed to Mlle. Peyronnet that they drive their two-cylinder car to Moscow. She wanted to see how the Russians were getting along with the building of Red Square, which she had visited in the nineteen-thirties. Since she did not want to be cooped up in a plane where she could not see anthing along the way, she decided they could take the car and sleep in it, as well as cook out to save money. Mlle. Peyronnet demurred, claiming her legs were too long to curl up in such a tiny vehicle.

Time was running out but Alexandra refused to recognize it. Two of her explorer friends in their sixties wrote they were coming to see her. Excited and pleased, she ordered Mlle. Peyronnet to prepare tea and everything else to perfection. She took great pains with her appearance and, said her friend M. Monod-Herzen, was charming, hospitable and "tres coquette" during their visit. But as soon as the men left she asked for the window to be opened to let out the musky smell, exclaiming disappointedly, "They are old men!"

In her second-floor study lined with bookshelves, Alexandra

worked at her big desk on new books, wrote introductions to new editions of her old ones and carried on a vigorous business correspondence. In an adjoining room was a comfortable old armchair where she slept, read, and admired the view of the mountains. When she had passed her 100th birthday her English editor, John Robinson, paid her a visit. He expected to find a wise old woman meditating and preparing for her death. Instead he found a canny bargainer familiar with every clause and percentage of her contracts. She wanted to negotiate with him to forego the royalties on the translations of her books and get instead a big advance immediately.

In the last half of her life Alexandra David-Neel enjoyed herself enormously, never making much of the dangers and hardships of her explorations. In the same spirit she dismissed the infirmities of age to concentrate on her intellectual interests and relish the recognition she had lived long enough to receive in full measure. Her third promotion in the Légion d'Honneur, to a Premier Commandeur, was presented to her at a ceremony in Digne, May 1964, when she was ninety-four years old. She wore a beautiful silk Tibetan robe and her white hair was swept up into a neat chignon on top of her head. Her eyes were very bright and her lips pursed in a puckish grin. She may have been thinking of the words she wrote nearly forty years earlier:

> Some will think that I have been uncommonly lucky. I shall not disagree; but luck has a cause, like anything else, and I believe there exists a mental attitude capable of shaping circumstances more or less according to one's wishes.

Alexandra David-Neel died peacefully at Samten Dzong on September 8, 1969, seven weeks short of her 101st birthday.

EPILOGUE

THERE IS NO EVIDENCE that the thirst to travel is genetically limited to males. Yet women travelers and explorers have been regarded as unimportant eccentrics or anomolies devoid of the heroic qualities possessed by their male counterparts. Pioneer wives, mothers and daughters could be valorous in support of their husbands and children. But pioneer women travelers have not been allowed an honorable tradition.

Women whose curious and restless spirits compelled them to travel alone were too far removed from their traditional roles to be taken seriously. They evoked laughter—sometimes gentle, sometimes derisive. They were regarded as unfulfilled females. Had they been seeking sexual adventures and ridden off into the desert with a dashing Arab sheik in the tradition of Lady Ellenborough, then romance was served. Love in an exotic setting was understandable. Of if they escaped the conventional life by attaching themselves to a man and exploring the mysteries of other cultures in the manner of Isabel Burton, whose passion for the famed Victorian traveler Sir Richard Burton was first fired by accounts of his exploits in Arabia, then that, too, was comprehensible. What was incomprehensible was a woman seeking high adventure for any motive other than love.

Male adventurers have been mavericks. But they could justify their flights from society by making scientific or mountaineering expeditions or single-handed journeys of courage and endurance. Their bravery, vision and daring validated those qualities in all men. The female adventurer was outside any feminine tradition. Her exploits were treated as individual aberrations unrelated to the conditions or needs of any other women.

Voyages have served in literature as metaphors for self-discovery. Adventure stories, beginning with the myths, folktales and epics, are a celebration of the search for a meaning of life. The tradition persists from Homer, Virgil and Dante through Swift, Conrad and Malraux. Each hero has a tale to tell that enlarges the vision and enhances the possibilities for action in every listener.

While most travelers do not self-consciously set out in search of themselves, they often find, if they explore beyond the well-worn paths, that they are less surprised at unfamiliar sights than they are astonished by themselves. A person's steadfastness and ingenuity are tested by the rigors of serious travel: inevitably there are frustrations of plans, sudden crises, tedium and hardship. When pitted against the forces of nature one's physical limits are defined. In an alien culture one's values are challenged. The farther women travelers dared to go the more they found within themselves qualities not encouraged in their upbringing.

Pregnancies and centuries of conditioning had kept women in an exceedingly narrow domestic world. So when the Victorians sallied forth they made some startling discoveries about themselves. They learned that they were physically tough—even the small ones like Annie Taylor, Isabella Bird Bishop and Alexandra David-Neel. And they were not burned out by the time they were thirty years old as Freud declared all women were. Fanny Bullock Workman made her greatest feat of exploration when she was fifty-three. Alexandra David-Neel was fifty-six when she walked 2,000 miles to Lhasa. And Isabella Bishop rode horseback 1,000 miles across Morocco in her seventieth year. The unexpected joy of physical triumph is voiced again and again in women travelers' books. Jane Duncan, a Scotswoman who left no record of her life except one delightful book (modestly titled, *A Summer's Ride Through Western Tibet* 1906,), is a typical example. When she crossed the Chang La, a 17,670-foot pass, she wrote, "I felt the air so exhilarating that I could have laughed and sung from pure joy if there had been anyone to keep me in countenance, and I was in the saddle for seven and a half hours continuously that day without feeling tired." Later she gave her account of crossing the Chang La "to a literary friend to read, and his criticism," she said, "was that I did not harp sufficiently on the agonies of the journey; but as I did not suffer any agonies, I do not quite see how the harping is to be done. At the time it seemed throughout an easy, common-place affair which anybody could have accomplished, and I have no gift of fine writing to cast a glamor over it and make it appear the tremendous achievement it was not."

Elizabeth Kendall, a lecturer at Wellesley College, Massachusetts, shared Jane's diffidence. She and Jane met briefly in Leh, Ladakh, when each was traveling alone through Little Tibet. Then in 1911, still "under the spell of the Orient," Elizabeth turned eastward again and traveled from Haiphon up through Western China and across the Gobi Desert to Siberia where she boarded the Trans-Siberian railroad near Lake Baikal. She wrote a book about the trip: *A Wayfarer in China* (1913). "Of course I was told not to do it," she recalled, "but that is what one is always told. A solitary summer spent . . . among the Himalayas of Western Tibet gave me heart to face such discouragement. I had no difficulties, no adventures, hardly enough to make this tale interesting." What did upset her was that "A request for some bit of information so often met with no facts, but simply the stern remark that it was not a thing for a woman to do."

Elizabeth passed through Tatsienlu, the Chinese Tibetan city that Isabella Bishop longed to visit, where Annie Taylor was sent out of Tibet and where Alexandra David-Neel lived during her last years in China. There Elizabeth spent an enjoyable evening with the English Captain F. M. Bailey, who was on his way to

Tibet. He did not reach Lhasa, she learned later, but he won the Gill medal from the Royal Geographical Society for his explorations. In their comparison of experiences, Elizabeth "was impressed, as often before, by the comfort a man manages to secure for himself when traveling. If absolutely necessary, he will get down to the bare bones of living, but ordinarily the woman, if she has made up her mind to rough it, is far more indifferent to soft lying and high living, especially the latter, than the man." The women travelers were exhilarated by their stamina but could not cast themselves as heroes. Daring adventure tales were not their genre.

But the more women traveled alone the more they were able to shed their inhibiting feminine self-consciousness. Nina Mazuchelli was so bound by the expectations and accouterments of her culture she could scarcely walk. She felt it was wildly unconventional to wear mocassins. But Isabella Bird Bishop, from that day in California when she stashed her skirt in a corn bin and swung astride a saddle, felt confident enough to select her dress more for comfort and freedom than fashion. And Alexandra David-Neel was able to shed the role of a Western woman altogether to adopt disguises like many of the great male travelers.

One of the delights that women travelers discovered was the pleasure of decision-making. At home they seldom had the opportunity. Out in the world, alone, every move was up to them; and after such freedom it was hard to go home again. Wives, mothers, and daughters rarely exercised such complete control over their own actions. Jane Duncan explained the joys of being responsible to oneself alone: "One of the luxuries of traveling alone is being free to change one's plans at any moment . . . The feeling of being able to turn back naturally did away with the wish for it—naturally so in the case of a woman at least." Later, when Jane Duncan met a Miss Christie in a valley in Kashmir, "We agreed as to the joy there is in traveling alone." They made a pact to strike their camps on different days so that they would not overtake each other on the trail.

If more women travelers had written confidently about their

joy and success they might have established a talismanic source from which others could draw strength. It was news in Victorian times, as it still is today, that women have the same range of psychological abilities to cope with dangers and difficulties that men do; that a number of them have impressive physical endurance; that some experience exhiliration testing their limits; and, most unorthodox of all, that women, like men, can simply have fun being adventurers and explorers—self-reliant and sometimes alone. It is probable that women travelers were so diffident about their discoveries because they saw themselves as society did—odd and irrelevant. They were isolated. They did not know how to support and commemorate each other.

But the early women travelers were not trivial. As their education improved they moved from an amateur to a professional point of view. Limited as all human beings are by their cultures, these women nonetheless refused to be shaped entirely by the external forces of society. They were rebels with dreams and the drive to realize them.

Without encouragement or examples to guide them these early travelers simply packed their bags and set out to see the world. It proved to be far less formidable than they had been led to believe. In fact, for women with adventure in their hearts the experience of being on their own was like a potent elixir of life. Traveling, like studying, was the true fountain of youth, said Alexandra David-Neel. For "travel not only stirs the blood . . . it also gives strength to the spirit."

NOTES

Nina Mazuchelli

1. Gillian Avery, *Victorian People*, p. 156.

2. Philip Woodruff, "The District Officer," in *The Guardians*, pp. 91–97.

3. Alstair Lamb, *Britain and Chinese Central Asia*, pp. 87–102. Dr. Joseph Hooker a distinguished naturalist and Dr. A. Campbell, a British Superintendent of Darjeeling, made their botanical expedition to Sikkim in 1849. Their capture was a famous incident in British-Tibetan relations on the northern border of India. Lamb treats it more fully than most historians. He acknowledges that Campbell's interest in Sikkim was political and that he had the "occupational disease" of wanting to visit Tibet shared by most British officials along the frontier. He cites an entry in Campbell's diary on his departure to Sikkim: "I can scarcely believe that I am really *en route* for Tibet. For twenty years it has been a primary object of my ambition to visit that land, of which so little is really known." pp. 94–95.

4. John MacGregor, "The Pundits," in *Tibet*, pp. 251–277.

5. Dr. C. Willet Cunnington, "The Ornamental '70s" in *Feminine Attitudes*, pp. 201–236.

6. Percival Spear, *The Nabobs*, pp. 140–143; Philip Woodruff, *The Founders*, p. 383. Spear is a principal advocate of the argument that the arrival of Englishwomen in India was a major cause of the social estrangement between the English and the Indians. He states flatly that nothing "ever tempted" Englishwomen to abandon "their insular whims and prejudices." Woodruff is the only historian I know to challenge the existence of a golden age of social intercourse between Englishmen and Indians. His documented position is that contrary to popular opinion Indian mistresses, often called "sleeping dictionaries," did not significantly integrate Englishmen into Indian social life.

Mazuchelli, Elizabeth Sarah, *The Indian Alps and How We Crossed Them*, London, 1876. This book has been catalogued by the British Museum under Nina Mazuchelli. Now that the India Office records and the author's will have been consulted it is established that Nina's proper Christian names are Elizabeth Sarah. The BM has corrected its catalogue. Other libraries may not have done so.

Annie Royle Taylor

1. Abbé Huc, *High Road in Tartary*.

2. Graham Sandberg, *Exploration of Tibet*, pp. 210–213.

3. "The Origin of the Tibetan Pioneer Mission," *The Christian*, 17 August 1893, p. 6.

4. William Carey, *Adventures in Tibet*, pp. 146–150.

5. Isabel S. Robson, *Two Lady Missionaries*, pp. 11–104.

6. Kenneth S. Latourette, *A History of Christian Missions*, pp. 390–408.

7. Annie Martson, *The Great Closed Land*, p. 103.

8. Mildred Cable, *The Challenge of Central Asia*, p. 103.

9. W. W. Rockhill, *Mongolia and Tibet*. Rockhill reached Kumbum in 1889, two years after Annie Taylor. His expedition did not get as close to Lhasa as she did.

10. Carey, pp. 150–162.

11. Ibid, p. 164.

12. Ibid, pp. 167–169.

13. Robson, pp. 99–102.

Taylor, Annie Royle. "Diary of Miss Taylor's Journey (from Tau-Chau to Ta-Chien-Lu) Through Tibet." *Adventures in Tibet*. Ed. Wm. Carey. Boston: United Society of Christian Endeavor, 1901.
—, "An Englishwoman in Thibet." *National Review*, Sept. 1893, pp. 25–35.
—, "My Experiences in Tibet." *The Scottish Geographical Magazine*, Dec. 1893, pp. 1–8.
—, "The Tibetan Mission." *The Christian*, Aug. 17, 1893.
—, *Pioneering in Tibet: The Origin and Progress of "The Tibetan Pioneer Mission" Together With My Experiences in Tibet and Some Facts About the Country*. London: Morgan and Scott, (1895?).

Isabella Bird Bishop

1. Anna M. Stoddart, *The Life of Isabella Bird: (Mrs. Bishop)*, p. 149.

2. Ibid., pp. 9–12.

3. Ibid., p. 49.

4. Ibid., p. 74.

5. Pat Barr, *A Curious Life for a Lady*, p. 89.

6. Stoddart, p. 96.

7. Ibid., p. 97.

8. Barr, p. 185.

9. Stoddart, p. 197.

10. Dorothy Middleton, *Victorian Lady Travelers*, pp. 19–20.

11. Barr, pp. 219–254.

12. Stoddart, pp. 300–301.

13. Stodart Walker, "Mrs Bishop," *The Edinburgh Medical Journal*, Nov. 1904, p. 383.

14. Isabella L. Bird, *A Lady's Life in the Rocky Mountains* (Norman: University of Oklahoma Press, 1960), p. xviii.

Bird, Isabella L. *An Englishwoman in America*. London: John Murray, 1856.
—, *The Aspects of Religion in the United States of America*. London: Sampson Low, Son, & Co., 1859.
—, *The Hawaiian Archipelago: Six Months Among the Palm Groves, Coral Reefs and Volcanoes of the Sandwich Islands*. London: John Murray, 1875.
—, *Unbeaten Tracks in Japan: An Account of Travels on Horseback in the Interior Including Visits to the Aborigines of Yezo and the Shrines of Nikkô and Isé*. 2 vols. London: John Murray, 1880.
—, *The Goldon Chersonese and the Way Thither*. London: John Murray, 1883
Bishop, Isabella L. Bird. *Journeys in Persia and Kurdistan: Including a Summer in the Upper Karun Region and a Visit to the Nestorian Rayahs*. 2 vols. London: John Murray. 1891.
—, *Among the Tibetans*. New York: Fleming H. Revell Co., 1894.
—, *Korea and Her Neighbors: A Narrative of Travel, with an Account of the Recent Vicissitudes and Present Position of the Country*. 2 vols. London: John Murray, 1898.
—, *The Yangtze Valley and Beyond: An Account of Journeys in China, Chiefly in the Province of Sze Chuan and Among the Man-tze of the Somo Territory*. London: John Murray. 1900.

Fanny Bullock Workman

Epigraph. Janeway, Elizabeth. In *Man's World, Woman's Place*, New York: William Morrow & Co., 1971, p. 301.

1. Ronald Clark, "The Women," *The Victorian Mountaineers*, London, 1953, pp. 174–185. Clark points out that both the belief that mountain climbing was not a womanly occupation and the type of clothing worn in the 1880's hindered mountaineering among women. He chronicles some of the earliest women climbers in the Alps.

2. Colonel Sir Sidney Burrard, *A Sketch of the Geography and Geology of the Himalaya Mountains and Tibet* (Delhi: Geological Survey of India, 1933), p. 15. Sir Sidney, defending the Survey of India position, argues that geographical Tibet embraces Ladakh and the Karakoram mountains of Baltistan, from longitude 74° to 95°. Political Tibet denotes only the country under the government of Lhasa.

3. Ibid., p. 11.

4. Ibid., p. 197.

5. Sven Hedin, Chpt. XLIX, "Mr and Mrs Workman," in *Southern Tibet*, Vol. II of *The History of the Exploration in the Kara-Korum Mountains*. (Stockholm, 1922) pp. 441.

6. Annie Peck, "To the Editor," *Scientific American*, 26 Feb., 1910, p. 183.

7. Hedin, Chpt. LIII "The Expedition of Dr. and Mrs. Workman, 1911–1912," p. 485.

8. Kenneth Mason, *Abode of Snow* (New York: E. P. Dutton & Co., 1955), pp. 139–140.

9. Hedin, "Expedition," p. 486.

10. J. P. Farrar, "In Memoriam: Mrs. Fanny Bullock-Workman," *Alpine Journal*, May, 1925, p. 182.

11. Arthur W. Tarbell, "Mrs. Fanny Bullock Workman," *New England Magazine*, Dec., 1905, p. 182.

12. Farrar, p. 182.

Workman, Fanny Bullock and William Hunter. *Algerian Memories: A Bicycle Tour Over the Atlas Mountains to the Sahara*. London: T. F. Unwin, 1895.
—, *Sketches Awheel in Modern Iberia*. New York: G. P. Putnam's Sons, 1897.
—, *In the Ice World of the Himalaya: Among the Peaks and Passes of Ladakh. Nubra, Suru, and Baltistan*. London: T. Fisher Unwin, 1900.
—, *Through Town and Jungle: Fourteen Thousand Miles A-Wheel Among the Temples and People of the Indian Plain*. London: T. Fisher Unwin, 1904.
—, *Ice-Bound Heights of the Mustagh: An Account of Two Seasons of Pioneer Exploration and High Climbing in the Baltistan Himalaya*. London: Archibald Constable & Co., Ltd., 1908.
—, *Peaks and Glaciers of Nun Kun: A Record of Pioneer Exploration and Mountaineering in the Punjab Himalaya*. London: Constable & Co., Ltd, 1909.
—, *The Call of the Snowy Hispar: A Narrative of Exploration and Mountaineering on the Northern Frontier of India*. London: Constable & Co. Ltd., 1910.
—, *Two Summers in the Ice-Wilds of the Eastern Karakoram: The Exploration of Nineteen Hundred Square Miles of Mountains and Glaciers*. London: T. Fisher Unwin, Ltd., 1917.

Alexandra David-Neel

1. Jeanne Denys, *A. David-Neel au Tibet* (Paris: La Pensée Universelle, 1972). Denys claims that David-Neel's parents were Jewish. The librarian at the Alliance Israélite, 45 rue La Bruyère, Paris, where files are kept on all prominent Jews, confirmed that research has not been able to establish any Jewish ancestry for David-Neel.

2. Certificat de Baptême, Diocèse: Creteil, Paroisse Notre-Dame de Saint-Mandé, Baptême No. 59, Année 1868.

3. Alexandra Myrial, *Pour la Vie* (Bruxelles; Temps Nouveaux, 1902).

4. See David-Neel, *Secret Oral Teachings* for explanation of *tulka*, often incorrectly called "Living Buddha," pp. 104–107.

5. The order was sent by Chas. A. Bell, later Sir Chas, who wrote an English-Tibetan colloquial grammar and dictionary in 1905 which was reprinted several times, the latest edition by the West Bengal Government Press in 1965. Author of *The People of Tibet* (Oxford: The Clarendon Press, 1928), *The Religion of Tibet* (Oxford: The Clarendon Press, 1931), and *A Portrait of the Dalai Lama* (London: Collins, 1946).

6. Denys, *A. David-Neel au Tibet.*

7. In the Tibetan Department of the Musée de l'Homme, Paris, there is a box containing some of the clothes David-Neel wore on her journey to Lhasa which are all very worn and full of holes: a long full red wool skirt, a woolen jacket with bits of brocade, a heavy red wool vest, a white wool stocking cap with face openings, a cap bordered in lamb's wool and sun goggles.

8. See David-Neel, *Journey to Lhasa,* pp. 132–133 for the full account.

9. See F. Spencer Chapman, *Lhasa: The Holy City* (London: Chatto & Windus, 1938), for one of the most complete descriptions of the city so few Westerners have visited and which still is virtually inaccesible. Chapman was Private Secretary to the head of the British mission to Lhasa in 1936. While he was very censorious of the Tibetans for their lack of hygiene he was impressed with their greatest building. "Certainly," he declared, "the Potala is one of the most astonishing buildings in the world . . ." To him it had a "transcendent quality." p. 171–182.

10. David Macdonald, *Twenty Years in Tibet,* pp. 288–290. Macdonald's mother was Sikimese and he was bilingual in Tibetan and English.

11. Robert B. Ekvall, *Religious Observances in Tibet,* p. 255.

12. David-Neel, *Magic and Mystery in Tibet* (New York: Claude Kendall, 1932), p. vi.

13. William G. Sewell was a professor of chemistry at the West China Union University at Chengtu and heard David-Neel speak there.

Works in English
David-Neel, Alexandra. *My Journey to Lhasa: The Personal Story of the Only White Woman Who Succeeded in Entering the Forbidden City.* New York: Harper & Bros., 1927.
—, *Initiations and Initiates in Tibet.* London: John Rider and Co., 1931.
—, *With Mystics and Magicians in Tibet.* London: John Lane, 1931.

—, *The Superhuman Life of Gesar of Ling*, New York: Claude Kendall, 1934.
—, *Tibetan Journey*. John Lane, 1936.
—, *Buddhism: Its Doctrines and Methods*. London: John Lane, 1939.
—, *The Secret Oral Teachings in Tibetan Buddhist Sects*. Foreword by Alan Watts. San Francisco: City Lights Book, 1967. (The translation from the French was originally published by the Maha Bodhi Society in Calcutta in 1964.)

Works in French
David, Alexandra. *Socialisme Chinois: Le Philosophe Meh-Ti et L'Idée de Solidarité*. Londres: Luzac et Co., 1907.
—, *Grammaire de la Langue Tibétaine Parlée*. Paris, 1899.
—, *Les Théories Individualistes dans la Philosophie Chinoise*. Paris: Giard et Brière, 1909.
David-Neel, Alexandra. *Grand Tibet: Au Pays des Brigands Gentilshommes*. Paris: Plon, 1933.
—, *Le Modernisme Bouddhiste et le Bouddhisme du Bouddha*. Paris: Felix Alcan, 1936.
—, *Magie d'Amour et Magie Noire: Scènes du Tibet Inconnu*. Paris: Plon, 1938.
—, *Sous Des Nuées d'Orage: Récit de Voyage*. Paris: Plon, 1940.
—, *A l'Ouest de la Vaste Chine*. Paris: Plon, 1947.
—, *Au Cour des Himalayas: Le Nepal*. Paris: Editions Charles Dessar. 1949.
—, *L'Inde Hier—Aujourd'hui—Demain*. Paris: Plon, 1951.
—, *L'Inde Où J'ai Vécu: Avant et Après l'Indépendence*. Paris: Plon 1951.
—, *Ashtavakra Gîtà: Discours sur la Védanta odvaïta;* Traduit du *sanscrit*. Paris: Adyar, 1951.
—, *Textes Tibétains*. Paris: La Colombe, 1952.
—, *Le Vieux Tibet Face à la Chine Nouvelle*. Paris: Plon, 1953.
—, *Quarante Siècles d'Expansion Chinoise*. Paris: La Palatine, 1964.
—, *En Chine: l'Amour Universel et l'Individualisme Intégral; Les Maîtres Mo-Tsé et Yang-Tchou*. Paris, Plon, 1970.

EPILOGUE
Duncan, Jane E. *A Summer Ride Through Western Tibet*. London: Smith, Elder & Co., 1906.
Kendall, Elizabeth. *A Wayfarer in China*. Boston: Houghton Mifflin, 1913.

BIBLIOGRAPHY

TIBET

The literature on Tibet is surprisingly large for so remote and sparsely settled a country. Secrecy provokes inquiry and speculation, and undoubtedly accounts for Tibet's hold on both the scholarly and popular imagination. For an introduction to the country see Hugh E. Richardson's *Tibet and Its History* (Oxford University, 1962). Two excellent books, Alstair Lamb's *Britain and Chinese Central Asia: The Road to Lhasa (1767 to 1905)* (Routledge and Kegan Paul, 1960) and Robert B. Ekvall's *Religious Observances in Tibet: Patterns and Function* (University of Chicago, 1964) have extensive bibliographies. Ekvall was born in China and lived for a number of years in Tibet. His intimate knowledge of Tibetan life is rare among scholars. David Macdonald who was the British Trade Agent in Tibet and host to Alexandra David-Neel when she came out of Lhasa, wrote an interesting account of his life as it related to British affairs on the Indian subcontinent, titled *Twenty Years in Tibet* (Lippincott, 1932). Peter Fleming (brother of Ian Fleming, creator of James Bond) in *Bayonets to Lhasa* (Rupert Hart-Davis, 1962) gives a lively account of the British invasion of Tibet in 1904.

A Cultural History of Tibet (Weidenfeld & Nicolson, 1968) by David Snellgrove and Hugh Richardson is a beautifully illustrated erudite book. More readable is the autobiography of the brother of the Dalai Lama: *Tibet Is My Country* (Rupert Hart-Davis, 1960) by Thubten Norbu.

Among the books that cover the principal explorers the most useful are *The Exploration of Tibet* (Delhi, 1904, reprint, Cosmos Publication, 1973) by Graham Sandberg, *Tibet, the Mysterious* (New York: Frederick Stokes & Co., 1906) by Col. Sir Thomas H. Holdich and *Tibet, A Chronicle of Exploration* (Praeger, 1970) by John MacGregor.

WOMEN TRAVELERS AND EXPLORERS

Of the five women covered in this book only one has had biographies written about her. They are *The Life of Isabella Bird Bishop* (Dutton, 1908) by Anna Stoddart and *A Curious Life for a Lady* (Doubleday, 1970) by Patt Barr. Isabella Bird was included in two other books: *Celebrated Women Travellers of the Nineteenth Century* (London: W. Swan Sonnenschein & Co., 1883) by Wm. Davenport Adams and *Pioneer Women* (London: The Sheldon Press, 1930) by Margaret E. Tabor, as well as in Herbert Van Thal's *Victoria's Subjects Travelled* (London: Arthur Baker, 1951) an anthology that includes writings by ten more women. Isabel Robson wrote about Annie Taylor in *Two Lady Missionaries in Tibet* (London: S. W. Partridge & Co.). Annie Taylor's attempt to reach Lhasa inspired the other missionary Robson covered, Dr. Susie Rijnhart, who, with her husband tried to make a similar journey in 1894. Her infant son died and her husband was killed in Tibet, but Dr. Rijnhart went on alone through hostile country to China. Her account is *With the Tibetans in Tent and Temple* (Chicago: Fleming H. Revell Co., 1901). Dorothy Middleton in *Victorian Lady Travelers* (Routledge & Kegan Paul, 1965) wrote about Isabella Bishop, Annie Taylor and Fanny Bullock Workman with a slightly different perspective from mine: she admired their gumption but thought they were quaint.

For a chronicle of women missionaries in the Far East see *A History of Christian Missions in China* (Macmillian, 1929) by Kenneth S. Latourette. Another early traveler in Tibet was Mrs. Littledale who, with her husband, a big-gamehunter and explorer, attempted to reach Lhasa in 1895. Sir George Littledale's article about their ill-fated expedition was published in the *Royal Geographical Society Journal,* Vol. 7, 1896, "A Journey Across Tibet From North to South and West to Ladakh." Alicia Bewicke Little claimed to be the first European woman to visit Tatsienlu. Her high-spirited account, "A Summer Trip to Chinese Tibet" was published in the *Cornhill Magazine,* Feb. 1899. In the 1920's and '30s three itinerant missionary women traveled among the oases of the Gobi Desert. To return to Europe they chose to take the old trade route northwest past the Great Wall of China, through Mongolia and Siberia. One of them, Mildred Cable, wrote about their journey in *The Gobi Desert* (London: Hodder & Stoughton, 1942). Also in the thirties, Ella Maillart, a French journalist, made a remarkable trip across China and Tibet with the English reporter, Peter Fleming. Her book is *Forbidden Journey: From Peking to Kashmir* (Wm. Heinemann, 1937). His is *News From Tartary* (Jonathan Cape, 1936). More recently Dervla Murphy, a thirty-year-old Irishwoman set out from County Waterford and bicycled alone all the way, through Persia and Afghanistan, to India. Tibet was closed to her but she worked in the Tibetan refugee camps in the Indian Himalayas and wrote a lively, perceptive book about her experiences and the plight of the Tibetans: *Tibetan Foothold* (John Murray, 1966).

VICTORIAN WOMEN

Most of the descriptions of colonial life written by women were in the form of diaries and letters. Few were printed for other than private distribution. But for readers interested in Anglo-Indian life in the nineteenth century from a woman's viewpoint two delightful books are available in most libraries: Emily Eden's *Up Country* (London: R. Bently, 1866) and Lady Falkland's *Chow-Chow* (London: Eric Partridge, 1930). Both women were in very privileged positions but they traveled a good deal within India and were keen observers. And Maud Diver in *The Englishwoman in India* (Blackwell, 1909) gives a detailed account of women's roles in colonial life. For those fascinated as I am by the conduct of Westerners in Asia I recommend Percival Spear's *The Nabobs: A Study of the English in 18th Century India* (Oxford Paperbacks, 1963) and the very well written work, *The Men Who Ruled India:* Vol. I, *The Founders*; Vol. II, *The Guardians* (Jonathan Cape, 1963) by Philip Woodruff. Spear has an excellent bibliography and Woodruff extensive notes.

The current re-evaluation of the Victorian period has inspired a number of excellent books concerned either directly or indirectly with the position of women. Two good books to start with are *The Victorian Woman* (Stein & Day, 1972) by Duncan Crow and *Suffer and Be Still* (Indiana University, 1972) edited by Martha Vicinus. Dr. C. Willet Cunnington has been interested in the subject for a long time and written several books. His *Feminine Attitudes in the Nineteenth Century*, first published in 1935, was re-issued by Haskell House in 1973. An authority on Victorian social life who is always a pleasure to read is Gillian Avery. Try her *Victorian People* (Holt, Rinehart & Winston, 1970). Another delightful writer is James Laver whose several books include *Edwardian Promenade* (Houghton Mifflin, 1958), a light social history which has a chapter on women's clothes.

MEN AND THE EXPLORING INSTINCT

Theories abound about why men explore. Two recent books examine the impulse from different perspectives but both agree that it is rooted in the need for humans to define themselves in some larger terms than their own small lives. John R. L. Anderson in *The Ulysses Factor* (Harcourt, Brace, Jovanovich, 1970) writes about some modern explorers and has a chapter on women. Paul Zweig in *The Adventurer* (J. M. Dent & Sons, 1974) explores the values of adventure as extolled in literature from the earliest folklore to present-day writers such as Jean-Paul Sarte and Norman Mailer.

But nothing captures the flavor of adventure quite like first-hand accounts. Here of course men dominate the field. To appreciate the magnetism and uniqueness of Tibet the accounts of several early travelers should not be missed. The most famous is Abbé Huc's *Souvenirs of a Journey Through Tartary, Tibet and China During the Years 1844, 1845 and 1846*. An annotated edition by J. M. Planchet is published in two volumes by the Lazarist Press, Peking, 1931. But for a good quick read get Julie Bedier's abridged version *High Road in Tartary* (Chas. Scribner's Sons, 1948).

William Woodville Rockhill was an American diplomat in China whose explorations were partially sponsored by the Smithsonian Institution. See his *Diary of a Journey Through Mongolia and Tibet in 1891 and 1892* (Smithsonian Institution, 1894) and the Englishman, Captain Hamilton Bower's *Diary of a Journey Across Tibet* (London: Rivington, Percival & Co., 1894). The Orientalist who Alexandra David-Neel feared would publish before she did was Dr. Guiseppe Tucci whose *Secrets of Tibet* (Blackie & Sons, 1935) is a diary of his 1933 expedition to Western Tibet and *To Lhasa and Beyond* (Istituto Poligrafico Dello Stato, 1956) of his 1948 expedition. *In Silks, Spices and Empire* (Delacorte Press, 1968) the old China hands, Owen and Eleanor Lattimore, introduce and annotate a selection of first-hand accounts of travelers to Asia including Huc, Rockhill and Younghusband who led the 1904 British military expedition to Lhasa.

Finally there is no writer who captures the mysterious enchantment of Tibet better than Fosco Mariani particularly in *Secret Tibet* (Hutchinson, 1954) with an introduction by Bernard Berenson. His books have stirred the imaginations of modern adventurers I have known—women as well as men.

INDEX

The Author:

Born in Seattle, Luree Miller attended Reed College and Stanford University, where she received a B.A. in History in 1948. Her husband's foreign service career took her abroad for many years in Europe and Asia; upon her return to Washington, D.C. she earned an M.A. in Women's Studies at George Washington University. She is a member of the Author's Guild and the Society of Women Geographers. Now a freelance writer, she lives in Washington, D.C.

In addition to *On Top of the World,* Miller is the author of *Late Bloom: New Lives for Women,* and two children's books: *Gurkhas and Ghosts: The Story of a Boy in Nepal,* which was adopted by the Swiss government as a public school text, translated into French and German; and *Bala: Child of India,* selected by the British Institute of Race Relations as an outstanding contribution to international understanding, and translated into Hebrew by the government of Israel.

Other books from The Mountaineers include:

NAHANNI TRAILHEAD: A Year in the Northern Wilderness
By Joanne Ronan Moore. The Moores, newlywed Ontario teachers, built and lived a year in a log cabin in the wild, remote Nahanni Valley of Canada's Northwest Territory, with wolves and other creatures their only neighbors. *"Has the same charm and readability that exists in the journals of some of the early explorers."* —Quill & Quire

MILES FROM NOWHERE: A Round-the-World Bicycle Adventure
By Barbara Savage. Delightfully engaging story of a unique travel adventure—two years, 23,000 miles and 25 countries by bicycle. *"...a sprightly story that will appeal to any armchair traveler."* —Publishers Weekly. *"...extremely entertaining narrative."* —Library Journal. *"...a life-affirming book."* —Women's Sports

50 YEARS OF ALPINISM
By Riccardo Cassin. Autobiography of one of the world's great climbers, rich in anecdotes of climbing and climbers. This near-legendary Italian mountaineer's name is synonymous with some of the most important ascents in the history of the sport.

MOUNTAINEERING AND ITS LITERATURE
By W. R. Neate. Extensive, annotated bibliography on mountaineering works published in English since 1744. *"...heartily recommended."* —Choice

H. W. TILMAN: The Seven Mountain-Travel Books
One-volume compilation, unabridged, of the famed British explorer's mountain books: *Snow on the Equator, The Ascent of Nanda Devi, When Men and Mountains Meet, Mount Everest 1938, Two Mountains and a River, China to Chitral, Nepal Himalaya.*

MEN AGAINST THE CLOUDS
The conquest of Minya Konka ("Gongga Shan") in China in 1932 by Burdsall, Emmons, Moore and Young.

Write for illustrated catalog of more than 100 outdoor titles:
The Mountaineers • Books
306 2nd Ave. W., Seattle WA 98119